WHEN almost a hundred intelligent-but-angry teenagers and their teachers have to tell what they really think about each other and their failures, what do they say? What happens when the teacher demands war right in the classroom, and that war is openly declared and fought?

    ... explosion?

    ... or effective education?

For six years, the authors of *The Fourth R* experimented with just such an approach to the education of "drop-outs" who had failed to benefit from enrollment in some of America's best private and public schools. Their report on this experience explains much of what is really happening when sensitive, intelligent, yet suspicious young people refuse to come to terms with the educational systems imposed upon them.

The authors' quest for "the fourth R"—an effective approach for recovery of teenagers at odds with the educational processes—led to their founding of Remedial Scholastic Services, Inc., a very special school in Cambridge, Massachusetts. RSS openly accepted each student's art to the fullest, he gives prodigally from his own store of values... he feels eager to learn from students while he teaches them. If desperate students at RSS responded to such faith, teachers in regular schools would find it even more effective for those who are only temporarily wavering."

ABOUT THE AUTHORS

ROBERT B. HEINEMANN, a graduate of Swarthmore College, earned the degree of Master of Arts in Teaching at Harvard University. Marilyn Bernstein, who completed her undergraduate work at Cornell University, received a Master of Science degree in social work from Columbia University.

THE FOURTH R

THE FOURTH R

A Return to Learning
for Sidetracked Adolescents

BY ROBERT B. HEINEMANN

AND MARILYN BERNSTEIN

BEACON PRESS

Boston

To Our Own Children

☙ *Acknowledgments*

WE ARE DEEPLY GRATEFUL to Dr. Gordon Allport and the other Trustees of the Ella Lyman Cabot Trust and to Miss Katharine Taylor along with the other Trustees of the New World Foundation for their support and encouragement. We are especially thankful to Miss Taylor for her brilliant and imaginative approach to education. Her sympathetic interest in all who try to solve educational problems is unique.

We thank the professional people who gave us their time and expert opinions about the issues with which this book is concerned: Dr. Helen Beier, Chief Psychologist, Boston City Hospital Child Guidance Center, and Assistant Professor, Boston University Medical School; Dr. Graham Blaine, Psychiatrist, Harvard University Health Services; Dr. John Blitzer, Psychoanalyst, Cambridge, Massachusetts; Dr. William Crowell, Psychiatrist, Judge Baker Guidance Center, Boston; Dr. William Eger, Director, Boston City Hospital Child Guidance Center, and Assistant Professor, Boston University Medical School; Dr. Samuel Kaplan, Training and Supervising Psychoanalyst, Boston Psychoanalytic Institute, and Instructor, Harvard Medical School; Dr. Lowell Kingsley, Director, The Kingsley School, Boston; Dr. Joseph Lord, Psychologist, Children's Medical Center, Boston; Mr. Robert S. Parsons, Educational Counselor, Boston; Dr. Morris S. Schwartz, Professor of Sociology, Brandeis University; and Dr. William Stone, Assistant Psychiatrist, Children's Medical Center, Boston, and Instructor, Harvard Medical School.

Dr. Norman Bernstein suggested writing the story of the school, inspiring us to formulate ideas out of hunches and insights. This document exists because he gave us sympathetic, sound advice and tailor-made "psychotherapy" to sustain us when it seemed nothing else would.

vii

Mary Fassett Heinemann devoted herself to this manuscript, editing it with understanding and art. Every page has been shaped by her sense of style; her intelligence has clarified and extended every idea.

Most of all we are indebted to those former students and to parents of former students who answered questions completely and frankly when we asked them to help us gather and evaluate our materials. Our special gratitude is reserved for those who offered to contribute materials themselves.

Contents

❦ Epigraph

To begin with, my whole problem started when I was born. Things grew progressively worse as I aged, but it really began to sizzle when I left private school in 1961. I had been through so many private schools and left after that, that my parents decided to plant me in a public school. Now nothing against the Boston Public School System but I really didn't think that public schools were the thing for me. I finally got a little sick of it, and at the time I couldn't tell my parents a thing; conversation between us then was nothing more than 'It's a nice day out today' and similar small talk. My only solution was to quit the whole thing. . . . Somehow my father found out about RSS. He talked with Mr. H who talked with Mrs. Bee and that was that. I think, and sincerely hope that RSS did something.

A CONTRIBUTION FOR
The Fourth R FROM GEORGE, AGE 13

❦ Introduction

As EDUCATION HAS CHANGED from privileged opportunity to economic necessity, so has the "studious cloister's pale" of Milton become a vast, glassy airport where smooth young people arrive only to change planes and take off again. Efficient, well-dressed students crowd the terminal, keep their baggage at the proper weight, and maintain a respectful attitude toward the technicians. Yet there are laggards shuffling around the exits, the sort who always forget their luggage or their glasses and cannot, therefore, make their flights. Bright, even gifted, they still harbor aspirations, however little they advance. They stand a sullen and suspicious lot whose intelligence and sensitivity are, in an uninvestigated sense, outraged.

Schools, even when riding roughshod for efficiency and coverage, may recognize the oversight and add new services. The high school student can be "programmed" into costly developmental reading courses to speed him up. Later, he tries individual reading instruction. Or he may just go into the more economical Special Classes. But these are merely changes in strategy which do not offer a fresh start to an adolescent who questions the whole apparatus. His commitment to school learning is equivocal, and special help makes him feel still more trapped. With no faith in the so-called practical goals of education, he also turns away from its content. He brushes off the new methods as easily as he does improved gadgets, and doggedly courts failure. The next move is "theirs." And then it's "their" turn to feel outraged, and "they" sweep him and his problems into bins marked, "Unmotivated," "Intransigeant," "Unteachable," "Stupid," "Psychological." He disappoints his parents, teachers, and—most of all—himself.

In most large communities there are special remedial schools where these high school rejects can find one more chance. It was in such a remedial center in metropolitan Boston that we first worked together. The school followed orthodox remedial practices, the general educational convention; it abhorred negative thoughts. Those that came to the surface had to be soft-soaped back where they came from. The students' problems were squeezed into simple, prepared formulae for which, with ingenuity, teachers could work up easy drills, and some kind of sympathy. Every day the students were to have at least one academic success, and each his share of instant praise.

Yet these arrangements did not seem to help the really intelligent failures, with their persistently irritating way of never concentrating on any work and never paying serious attention to the most sympathetic interest. One day, a bright young fellow, "in" for a math disability, tore up his perfectly done test paper the instant he was praised for it. After this incident, both of us were ready for more curious "irregularities," and took our first steps into the forbidden wood of bad thoughts. Marilyn Bernstein, with experience as a psychiatric social worker and child therapist, began to speak up about the emotional dilemmas behind the failures; Bob Heinemann, experienced in guidance counseling and teaching, concentrated on the intellectual implications.

In the classroom we were uncertain about taking time to discuss reactions, time which had to be stolen from the assigned "teaching." Tutoring a single student gave more leeway and accented the student's need. Anger and fear often unveiled the way that private logic "justifies" learning disabilities which wash out bright minds. One small boy, in the face of all we could do, did not learn to read or write. Yet he knew how to draw accurately and to name the dinosaurs. Through those drawings and related discussions he made it clear that he suffered excruciating anxiety which was allayed only when his mother, holding him close in her lap, read to him. For him, learning to read would cost him too much; he had to fail.

Later, we were put in charge of the summer school and, being bolder, applied to the classroom group what we were learning from individual tutoring. We asked our group of six to talk over together with us what they felt and thought about the work that went so badly for them. Our academic objective was to show them how to read with better understanding and to write better compositions by allowing and encouraging an expression of whatever was uppermost in their minds. Suspicious at first, they threw up a barrier of clichés which had to be blasted down. As all this took large blocks of time, we ditched the rote drills and daily practice on machines. At the end of six weeks there were substantial improvements in test scores and the students were freer and livelier. We did not miss what we had jettisoned, and clearly the students did not.

Then the school was sold, and, prodded into action by job uncertainties, we established our own remedial school in Cambridge. That autumn we opened Remedial Scholastic Services, RSS. The name, neither easy nor pleasant to say, did not generally delight parents who were embarrassed about their children's shortcomings and preferred manorial or bosky-sounding school names. By calling a spade a shovel we addressed ourselves more to the students.

We began with five adolescent boys and one girl who had flunked out of college. Within two years we had an enrollment of 15 full-time students. The tuition was set at a forbidding $1,600 in an effort to make the school fiscally sound. There was a wide range in ages, for we included a number of children under twelve years old. We hired and trained teachers, and established tutoring and testing services for the use of regular schools and educational counselors in the area. Altogether about one hundred students came to RSS over a period of six years.

At the peak of our expansion a developed, systematic approach began to replace experimentation; and we saw more clearly the depths we had to probe, and indeed could probe as teachers, to effect radical changes in students. Afternoon and short summer-school tutoring programs, though leading to superficial improvements, were chiefly effective in putting off a serious approach to underlying problems. We decided to focus almost exclusively on small-group instruction, and gave up summer programs. Then, we discovered that while it was perfectly sound to treat the school problems of primary graders on the same basis as the others, we really preferred the company of adolescents, who needed less physical care. We set a lower age limit of twelve years, and from that time worked almost exclusively with high school and college students. Finally, we grew too large for our resources. Marilyn worked only part time, and the training and supervising of more teachers seemed to increase rather than relieve the strain. Under these circumstances we could not have the close relationships we wanted with our students, so we restricted our enrollment to eight carefully chosen full-time students.

The curriculum included mathematics, literature, history, languages, and composition. To teach students how to learn was our aim. The pace of this process was unimportant. Accordingly, we gave neither grades nor credits. Work followed current needs as the teacher saw them.

The underlying and persistent need for all our students was to disentangle emotional difficulties from academic life. Recognizing the importance each student gave to these disturbances was a step toward lending him support in sorting them out. However, that support was neither credible nor acceptable until we explained and deepened the relationship between him-as-student and us-as-teachers.

Feeling our way, we and the students analyzed the structure of our authority laid down as an unadorned social and psychological fact, that is, minus the paraphernalia of mechanistic rewards and punishments. Together we traced learning disabilities back to a matrix of fears and hostilities that had mushroomed in the dark when dissent had been either throttled or sweet-talked out of the classroom.

The process of exposing private scruples and long-hidden, dimly perceived dissidence was always difficult, and indeed terrifying with its threatened chaos and violence. Whether or not a creative teacher-student relationship could naturally and safely survive was one question. Whether, through such tempered relationships and the revival of dissent, learning disabilities might be prevented or conquered was another.

These pages introduce a variety of fictitious characters. While we would like readers to feel at home with them, none actually existed. We use real personality traits, statements and compositions verbatim, and true incidents, which are extracted from the whole range of our teaching during the entire period of our enterprise and are woven into composite characters and situations which we hope are plausible enough to illustrate typical developments. Seeking to portray a process rather than scheduling "things to do," we have allowed our "cast" to speak for themselves.

I ❧ *First Encounters*

RSS IS IN A RAMBLING CAMBRIDGE HOUSE, an ancient frame maze that laps up repairs only to settle back with its neighbors and look neglected anyway. The street-side porch and doorway are for us and the side entrance for the apartments upstairs. We have the downstairs three rooms and kitchen furnished with comfortable old household stuff supplemented by new steel-and-plastic desk chairs and green blackboards. The school office is a corner of the front room where a steel file stands guard over a rolltop desk and a telephone. A sofa backs up against the bay windows along the street and easy chairs hold down the empty corners. An air of long-suffering acceptance and crotchety gentility inside and out makes an easy backdrop, a neutral but not antiseptic setting for the interviews through which we choose our students.

Alden

Alden S. and his parents have come for just such an interview and are sitting in our "office." Alden at seventeen has been out of school for two years, though he has not finished the ninth grade. He sees a psychiatrist who a year earlier urged him to come to RSS, but Alden could not then bring himself to fill out an application. Now he has done so, and has also arranged this formal conference. He is a handsome, lively-looking boy, somewhat frail in body but vigorous in manner, all of which suggests sensitivity and intelligence. He smiles easily and is expensively and fashionably dressed, Ivy League style. An apparent affability and readiness to cooperate seem shining refutations of charges about serious problems. It is as if his school record, or rather his lack of one, should be taken as a kind of gentleman's joke.

"We don't know very much about you, Alden, except that you

6

haven't been in school for a while. I hope you won't mind if we start this interview by asking you why you want to go to school now."

Alden sits stiffly on a chair facing us and his parents, who are comfortably relaxed on the sofa. He looks at his father, who pulls on his pipe, saying nothing. His mother smiles. The buck is being passed.

It is easy to like Alden but hard to tell whether he can meet our standards. We are on the lookout for an ideal type of failure, an intelligent and somewhat emotionally depressed student, whose learning disabilities are sufficiently school-connected to be correctable in school. If he is not smart enough, everything moves too slowly; if, under stress, he resorts to impulsive action, he might be too destructive; if he is completely taken up with personal and family relationships, the periods when he totally blanks out on academic subjects will be too long. The trouble with standards like these is that it is hard to tell how any one person actually meets them all.

Prospective students usually are first introduced to us as "profiles," manila folders featuring school grades, isolated comments by past teachers, and test scores, to which there may be added, if a psychiatrist has had a hand in it, an account of emotional factors. As educators we are obliged to accept the manila folders, and they usually have some bearing on the problems we are interested in. But they tell us little about the internal resources students have, about their hearts and what they can give or what they must seize upon and take, about judgments and what makes them laugh, about ideals they are ashamed of having. Manila folders can enumerate aptitudes and achievements without ever recognizing real intelligence, much less those other, silent strivings. All this we hope to uncover in one short interview. Alden, of course, has such a slim folder that we have no alternative.

"I want to learn, I guess," Alden replies, when, after a long pause, no one else does.

"Didn't you want to learn before?"

His mother interrupts, "Oh yes, but it's always been hard for Alden to learn. He reads so slowly and haltingly. His spelling is incredible. I don't know what's wrong, but I think a lot of his trouble comes from bad teaching. Alden's first grade teacher—I remember her well—was just out of college and she was green. I don't think she had control of the class. But it wasn't only that. All the early grades use such boring books. Alden, or any other intelligent child would lose interest fast. I used to tell the teachers he was just too smart for them."

"Then Alden had school trouble for many years?"

"Well, yes, I guess so. I doubt if he ever liked school. And we've tried nearly all of them around here, don't you think so, Wally?" laughs Mrs. S, turning to her husband.

"Yes, dear. He's probably taking after his old man! I used to kid around in school quite a lot, and I never really liked it much. The boy is probably just the same. I couldn't even stay at Yale for four years! But at least I finished up by transferring to Trinity, and I graduated, by golly. I say Alden should put his shoulder to the wheel and give it everything he has. Why don't you get in there and try, son?"

Alden bristles for a moment and says sullenly, "C'mon, Dad. The more you lecture, the less I want to go to school."

"I don't understand, Alden. Did you stop going to school because your father lectured you?" I ask.

"No, but they're nagging me all the time."

"Alden, I really would like to know more about how you feel about school and why you left. Were you interested in any subjects?"

"Not really. Except science. I liked that a lot and . . ."

Mrs. S breaks in, "I think you have to understand how bad Alden's study skills are. Jim Treadwell the neurologist, you know, thinks there's something wrong with the way Alden sees things. I mean he reverses letters in his spelling and he's ambidextrous, too. Of course, I don't know whether I believe that has much influence. The truth is that Alden's smart as a whip and he knows it. He just won't be bothered learning anything that's dull. He knows how to charm teachers and change the subject."

"What made you decide to give up school?"

"I wasn't interested in it, especially when some of the teachers made sarcastic remarks about me. That made me mad. I guess they got annoyed because I overslept a lot. Anyway, I liked staying home for a while."

"How could you oversleep? Didn't you have an alarm clock?" pushes Marilyn.

"Of course he did," says Mrs. S. "Besides that, I used to call him in time for breakfast every morning. He just didn't seem to get up. After all, it's really up to him to get himself up. I used to think sometimes that he really loved to work on his car, and I thought he might as well be doing that as wasting his time doing absolutely nothing in school."

"Oh, you could have gotten me up, Mother. You were just too busy getting ready for your club meetings!"

"Now, son," intervenes Mr. S, "no need of that. I don't think Mr. Heinemann or Mrs. Bernstein is interested in a family squabble. We're here to see if you can come to school."

"There's no secret about it," continues Mrs. S. "We've tried everything with Alden, but he's always angry with me and his father. For two years he's been home making me wait on him. But now I don't let him hurt me."

"Alden, perhaps I should tell you something about the school, and then you can ask me some questions for a change. We're very small and everyone who comes here has a problem about schoolwork. What we want to do is to help students find out how to overcome their problems so that they can decide in their hearts whether they really want to go to school or not." Then I went on to explain the daily schedule, pointing out clearly the required and elective subjects.

"How old are the other kids?"

"Between thirteen and eighteen—usually high school students."

"Don't you have any science?"

"No, we haven't the facilities for teaching science, and anyway neither of us knows very much about it. But you said before that you used to like science, didn't you?"

"Uh huh. I really liked some of the projects they did in high school."

"What were they?"

"Well, there was one that was really fabulous. I mean it was really IT. Making artificial rubies. It was a project for the Science Fair."

"What marks did you get in science?"

"It was the one subject that I always passed. I guess I got C or maybe once a B."

"If you were interested in science, why didn't you do more work in it?"

"Oh, I wasn't really good at it! They probably would have laughed at my work in that class, too."

"Why, Alden, that's interesting. Before you didn't say that they laughed at you."

"Who laughed at you?" Marilyn asks.

"I can't remember."

"You must remember something, or you wouldn't have brought it up now."

"My math teacher made fun of me once. He was a sarcastic bird. He was probably laughing at me all the time."

"Why?"

"I don't know."

"Could you try to say? You must have a guess or an opinion about why he made fun of you."

"I said, I don't know."

Alden looks down at the floor, and says nothing further. Mr. and Mrs. S seem both amused and disgusted, but neither speaks.

Marilyn says, "It might be very important to know what you think about why teachers behave the way they do. I'd like to know why you are silent just at that point. So often you have answers at the tip of your tongue.

"You see, Alden, we will be bringing out things like this because usually kids lose interest in the schoolwork after a while. Then we'll ask why. It's crucial for you to know, if you don't now, what makes you 'turn off' learning. If you do know, it's important for you to express your feeling in words. Our idea is that if you can come out with such feelings and then discuss them, you may find a better way to deal with them than by wrecking your schoolwork, as you've done in the past. Of course, all this depends upon whether you really want to do something about your school troubles."

Alden looks quickly around at everyone, and then down at the floor again. His ready smile has deserted him. His lips curve scornfully, and he mutters in a monotone, "I'll bet you'd laugh at me, too. I don't know but you'd probably stick together just like the rest of my teachers."

"We are teachers, Alden. But we're not trying to prove we are right and you are wrong. We are trying to help you find out what has gone wrong in school for you, but we can't do much if you won't tell us the score. The only way you can find out for sure about our motives is to try us and see. As I said before, the whole thing depends upon whether you want to straighten yourself out about school enough to take a chance."

"I really *do* want to study and learn because I'd like to be a lawyer. Then I have to finish high school and go on to college. How many kids my age will there be?"

"There won't be very many. I can't be sure just now who will be coming, but there certainly will be some students younger than you."

"How much younger?"

"They will be around thirteen or fourteen."

"Ugh! I was sure I'd at least be with kids my own age. I'd be sort of embarrassed anyway to come to a place like this. I don't want to go to a school to talk about my problems, because I have to do that with my doctor. I just want to learn something and go to school with kids my own age."

"But I thought you left high school because you were embarrassed by your inability to do the work. Didn't you say that?"

"No, I didn't say that exactly."

"Isn't that part of what made you leave school?"

"Yes, but I still don't want to go to school with a bunch of children!"

"You shouldn't come here if you don't want to. It never works unless the student decides that he has learning problems that he wants to solve. If you're not really concerned enough to work hard on that you shouldn't join us."

"I didn't say I wasn't."

"Well, if you do want to solve them, we believe you have to learn how to face your problems openly, to know what they are. Do you think after two years at home you would actually be able to go right back to regular school and pick up your work without solving the problems you had when you stopped?"

"No. I know I do need help."

Mrs. S, keeping her amused look says, "If you spend so much time talking and trying to find out things—especially from *him*—when will you have time for getting him caught up in his reading and writing? That's where he needs to concentrate his time."

Marilyn then replies to Mrs. S, "We've found that students as bright as Alden can catch up easily when their minds are free from blocks that interfere. Once free, the student finds for himself how to learn. By that time he accepts help and guidance from a teacher. I don't think Alden has much tolerance for it now."

"When a student is not doing the assigned work, we always interrupt the class to talk. We may spend the rest of the hour discussing his reasons."

Mrs. S looks skeptical, "I hardly think that sounds—"

Mr. S asks, "What about homework? Do you assign much?"

"It depends. We only assign homework when we think a student can and should do it. I imagine in Alden's case we would not assign any, at least until we got to know him better."

Mrs. S explodes, "I think Alden should have plenty of work to do. Heavens, what will he do with the rest of the day if you don't give him homework? He's been idle long enough! I appreciate your point of view, but I'm beginning to think your school is a little too special."

Alden has been darting looks at his parents and us; his own expression warms up.

"I think I'd like to come here. I have problems, that's for sure, but I'd like to sort of forget about them. I guess I see that I can't do that." Irrepressible glee sweeps across his face. "I like the idea of no homework. When I'm at home I like to work on my Ford. It's a '28, you know."

"Are you more interested in your car than in getting back to regular school? You said you wanted to be with kids your own age again," I remind him.

"I do. But I've got to get that car on the road. We're going to have a rally in six weeks."

"Suppose we think you should do algebra homework, for example, and you want to work on your car instead. What will happen?"

There is a heavy silence.

"I don't know. Probably I'd work on the car."

"Well, Alden, that's a fair answer; and as things are now I can understand why you would prefer the car. But would you consider the conflict between car and school something to talk about, to find a different solution, perhaps?"

"I suppose so. As long as you don't try to get my parents to take the car away."

"Alden, one more thing. Why did you suddenly change your mind a few minutes ago? Earlier in the interview you said you didn't want to come here because of the younger students. But when your parents began to express their doubts about the school, you seemed to change your mind very quickly. What happened?" asks Marilyn.

"I guess I could say that I did it to go against my father and mother," Alden replies promptly.

"Yes, you could say that. But I don't think that's the only reason. I think there's something else. Will you tell us?"

"You mean about not having to do homework?"

"Something more than that."

"I don't know what you mean, Mrs. Bernstein."

"I mean, something positive happened, too. I think you liked something about us and our school. You learned something from this interview."

"No. You're wrong. I just changed my mind. That's all."

"Well, Alden, I don't agree. If we were in school right now, I would press you to explain your change of mind more fully and more openly. Do you think you could tolerate that kind of probing?"

"Well, I can't tell you that. I haven't anything more to say. I would like to come here and start school again."

I say, "OK. It's been a long session tonight. Why don't we all think about it? You have a lot to discuss, and we certainly want time to figure out whether we can really help you, Alden. If you decide that you want Alden to come, Mr. S, please call his doctor and the high school to authorize them to give us information about him. If you have any questions, we'd be glad to try to answer them."

Marilyn says, "Now, Alden. Don't make a hasty decision. I've been admiring you this evening for answering a lot of tough questions and in front of us all. I think you must have felt a little as though you were on trial and you handled it very well. If you decide to come, I'd like the chance to work with you."

"You mean you want him?" Mrs. S looks incredulous.

"Yes, but Mr. Heinemann and I ought to talk it over to be as sure as we can be that we will be able to help."

"You mean maybe he's beyond help?" asks Mr. S cheerfully.

"No. But there is always a question whether our particular program is suited to the needs of an individual. We don't like to waste his time or ours."

There are plenty of reasons for hesitation. The parents seem supercilious and cold, and their careless bromides are offensive; it is hard to imagine having good relations with them. Alden is too slick, and his change of heart in the interview puzzles us more than we said. But he is intelligent and full of humor, and the family as a whole seems to have a kind of animal vigor that ought to be something to build on. We like him, and feel sorry for him and decide to take a chance.

Matt

A shaggy eighteen-year-old sits across the room in our office, telling us he might come to RSS. He chats sociably, touching on reading speed, but he is evasive about his problems. Suave mannerisms, deferential "sirs," and restless digressions do not conceal his angry contempt.

"I'm living not far from here with my sister and a couple of her friends. The house is an awful mess and the owners are coming back next week! I don't know how to study. I think it's because I'm not reading enough, don't you, Mrs. Bernstein? Can you teach me to read faster, sir? I really want to . . . Oh, I like to read, but I must read too slowly because I haven't finished anything on my own for more than a year . . . The main thing is that I can't concentrate on my studies and so I don't get through my work. No, I don't think I want to look at my attitudes or the deep, deep reasons with you. I have my doctor for that, and I just want you to fix up my studies. Of course I'm terribly interested in the theater. I don't go to plays exactly, but just now I'm writing one about Dylan Thomas and one of his followers who tries to get Dylan to abandon what I call the realm of abstract generalizations for ROMT. That's the Realm of Materialistic Trivia. Too many people are ROMT. That's what I say, don't you think so? Of course Dylan never falls for it. What do you think of the idea, sir? Do you think you could help me with my reading problem? My parents come here sometimes, but they're usually pretty busy seeing friends."

This is Matt. Thin, out at the elbows in a stained corduroy jacket, sockless, bearded, and neglected, his learning problems are as vague as his clothes. Unlike many seeking remedial help, he loves to write and talk, though he cannot or will not study.

Sent East to boarding school at twelve, Matt infrequently covers the two thousand miles or so to go home these days. With a high I.Q., a fair scholastic record in his manila folder, his transfers from school to school were for social reasons rather than academic advancement. He is a senior at a well known preparatory school, editor of the school paper, and counselor in charge of younger students in his dormitory. However, important changes have been taking place. He is no longer passing in all subjects, and he wants to withdraw from school altogether because he cannot study. Persistent infractions of minor rules have been making the school administration uneasy, and the headmaster recommends a change. "The family," he commented, "is a fine one, and the boy deserves another chance. Something about him antagonized the teachers here. He's not remedial. He only needs part-time help with his school work. A little time to straighten himself out, and he'll be all right." Matt thinks he needs more than time, applying to us for help this summer when he and some other youngsters are living in a house "borrowed" from friends of his parents.

We do not know when we can meet Matt's parents. His father, a corporation executive tied up in Washington, has authorized his secretary in Denver to issue a check to pay for whatever arrangement we reach with Matt. His mother, shuttling between Denver and New York, London, or Paris, where their friends are, cannot change her plans but sends Matt her blessings.

Entering adolescence with support from home limited to the financial, Matt lives in a world of vague boundaries, full of fears about himself and his future. He is preoccupied with a thousand personal problems to which learning in school seems irrelevant. Enervating doubts about the goals of education stem from his taking it for granted that school responsibility is largely a social maneuver. He thinks he will wear the mantle of culture while others do the work of education.

Still, the clouds of pretension and the ravages of neglect have not smothered his gifts or intelligence, nor have they driven away all seriousness. He applies himself industriously to psychotherapy; and his psychiatrist, the only person in charge, thinks we should work with him. Matt has already rejected a late invitation to return to his regular school because he insists on finding his own goals. It is our impression that his questioning of education is sincere. We enroll him.

Phil

Phil is a nineteen-year-old veteran of testing services, educational counseling, and special schools of all kinds. He is an academic loser who seems unable to quit. His scores on tests have never been higher than the sixth grade level, while the estimates of his intelligence inside the manila folder are low, bordering sometimes on the defective. He must always have been a likable boy to whom no one has had the heart to say, "Stop! Get out of the academic line and try something else!" Each of many schools kept him for a year or until the discrepancies between physical and mental development became embarrassing; then another school was recommended somewhat along the lines of his first boarding school, who, in passing him along to the next, said, "A nice, well-mannered, very presentable boy who ought to be in a school where he could get more individual attention of the remedial sort." The last of the boarding schools dismissed him after six months with a curt, "We are not the right school for Phil." The special schools said more time was needed and complained that Phil did not do enough work at home and could not concentrate in school.

Phil and his mother come to the interview in a confident, jovial mood, as if it were a party. She is a wide-eyed, good-time blonde who looks at her son sometimes affectionately, and sometimes flirtatiously. He is tall with a nervous manner obscured by a lively smile and a ready deference. A hard, jewel-like glitter occasionally peeps through his good-natured sparkle, but what really jars is his fuzzy pink sweater.

Phil is neither ashamed of all the changes in school nor embittered. He is satisfied that they were too hard for him, but he is sanguine about his prospects with us. The last boarding school expelled him, he admits, because he was suspected of having an affair with the headmaster's daughter. Phil's mother giggles, and moves nervously on her seat. Phil says he has no desire to learn any more than he needs for going to work in his father's store and eventually running it. His mother says she wants him to finish high school, but knows he does not have the potential for college. Phil seems to be open and articulate about what he wants to do, and is obviously socially adept enough to be a competent salesman. It seems safe to assume that he has enough intelligence to master the three R's for his practical purposes. He has a vitality and responsiveness that makes us think we could help him. Yet, his fuzzy pink sweater and the exchange, sometimes, of coy glances with his mother give weight to certain doubts.

We cannot discuss serious educational questions without turning back to the frequent changes of school. Phil's mother admits after too much hedging that she divorced Phil's real father and re-married when Phil was only ten. All references to father really mean stepfather. Phil's sparkle fades, and his face looks vacant and hard. He repeatedly strikes his right fist against the open palm of his left hand. At last he jumps to his feet, strides out of the room into the kitchen in the back, and turns on the water tap. His mother smiles and explains in a confidential voice that Phil uses his stepfather's surname because he hates his real father and his name too. Phil's movements are no longer audible to us in the front room, and, with some concern, we look at the doorway through which he disappeared. It is a shock to see him peering round the edge of the door frame as if he were eavesdropping on a private conversation.

When we speak to him, he shuffles in with a contrite, sheepish expression. His mother chides him for his "silliness" until he looks boldly up at her and winks broadly. She giggles again, and together they burst into laughter. To us it is not a spoof but a serious action which needs a serious explanation, and we ask for one. Phil starts to reply; then, seeming to be forgetful, asks us to repeat our question. At last he shrugs his shoulders and looks truly bewildered as if he is too simple to understand. Yet, his face, when he concentrates on a question, seems to express fear. He gives up with a smile as if to say it really is better not to know. When we ask about psychiatric evaluations, his mother breaks in laughingly to say that they, too, have given him up. Phil is on his feet again, and pacing the floor. He adds a descriptive comment or two, but seems very agitated. He stops in front of the door, and stands listening to his mother. Suddenly he turns and with a balled-up fist savagely wallops the door panel. After a moment, he relaxes and grins, saying, "Don't ask me why I did it. It seemed like I wanted to, that's all. It's OK, isn't it? The door's OK." His mother orders him to sit down beside her and stop being foolish. They look at us expectantly, faces wreathed in smiles and good will.

Phil has genuinely appealing qualities, and he almost manages to make good-natured avoidance of problems seem seductively innocent and simple. But his restlessness and impulsive physical blows under nervous tension point to a brittle control overlying the violence. The feverish gaiety of mother and son along with their sly intimacy foretell a tempest of unpredictable savagery. Phil's dramatic demonstration of infantile eavesdropping is as uncomfortably incongruous as the fuzzy pink sweater. Obviously he is beset with urgent problems taking priority over the academic ones. To focus Phil's mind on academic questions would involve explosive confrontations probably way beyond the limits we have set for ourselves in school. Regretfully we turn down his application.

Jimmy

Jimmy is a teen-ager, a somewhat sullen, quickly defiant adolescent who has been in trouble over school discipline and even with the local police in his suburban shore-town. He is a slender sixteen-year-old, scrubbed and clean in tight, freshly creased chinos and an open shirt. His blond hair is brushed and shaped into an elaboration of the familiar duck's ass haircut, popular among teen-agers everywhere. Jimmy comes to our interview with his mother; the father, described to us as an ambitious, self-made engineer very recently promoted to an important executive post in a large factory, sends his regrets. Jimmy's mother is a small, mousy, conventional-looking woman whose initially intense fearfulness slowly leaks away during the interview, until, near the end, she gives a sympathetic account of herself and her son.

Jimmy tells us his sudden departure from high school began in a dispute over haircuts. The guidance counselor allegedly insisted on a more conservative style, and Jimmy, stung by this "invasion" of his personal domain, spoke sharply about the guidance man's baldness. Words and soon blows were traded. Although Jimmy insists he struck back in self-defense, the family decided to have him change schools.

Jimmy's version hardly refers to academic failure, but his mother complains about it, and the manila folder has details. He has never done well in school, but after only one term in the ninth grade his marks became consistently F. However, his achievement test scores were at the eleventh grade level in reading and the ninth in arithmetic, and his I.Q. was considered to be at least high average. It was reported, "His big trouble is wrong associates . . . He's a wise guy who sleeps in class when he isn't disturbing it. He doesn't listen, and that's why he can't learn . . . He needs to be pushed, but the trouble is that when he's pushed, he becomes hostile." Right now he glowers at us for discussing his school record. An habitual pout gives his face a petulant look anyway, but now his eyelids droop, he colors deeply, and obviously petulance turns to fury. He seems easily overwhelmed with feeling, and almost proud of his belligerence; yet he is not out of control.

Truculence combined with a history of impulsive behavior are against our taking him on. Moreover it appears that we might have to tune in on a kind of teen-age, rock-and-roll world where the prize is not maturity but perennial youth. Jimmy reminds us of those restless anti-adults of the youth gangs who, shunning culture as unmanly, yet want desperately to be "regular," their so-called rebelliousness never crimping an eagerness to be vulgar, that is violent, insensitive, and sentimental. Jimmy has many appealing qualities, but this aspect of his character puts us off.

Fortunately his folder gives us grounds for optimism. The educational counselor who referred the family to us, sensing the kind of problems behind Jimmy's behavior, persuaded Jimmy to consult a psychotherapist as part of a repair program. The psychiatrist has made his evaluation and agreed to work with Jimmy, basing his prognosis on facts we could not discuss in the interview. He said that Jimmy, at the age of five, had undergone a successful but very dangerous surgical removal of a tumor which at the time had stimulated a precocious sexual development. After the operation, his body returned to the state of a normal five-year-old. As his father was demanding and overcompetitive, the doctor concluded that Jimmy must then have been in the midst of the oedipal struggle. This was, he added, also the time when he began to go to school. Therefore, when castration fantasies were probably already assailing the boy, they seemed to find a confirmation in the reality of a frightening operation and a long stay in the hospital. Thus were later school problems lined up, predictably ready to break out when Jimmy reached normal adolescence. A rerun of the same psychological problems was pushing Jimmy down the path of juvenile delinquency. His reactions to teachers were rebellious, like his reactions to all father-surrogates, because of his terror of his real father. A coordinated therapeutic and educational approach could help Jimmy overcome such fears about growing up. It was a safe guess that Jimmy would not present serious behavior problems in a school where his psychological problems would be sympathetically understood.

In our interview Jimmy shows us that he is also worried lest the results of his school failure be permanent, as if not ready to give up on school. Yet, he does not seem ready to abandon his defiant attitude. He is obviously intelligent and speaks crisply and to the point in his own self-defense. He listens carefully and, with his watchful, hooded eyes, seems to observe everything. He says he wants to enter psychotherapy as well as work on his school problems with us. When we probe into his motives and challenge his statements, his interest quickens and he blushes more frequently. He is responsive, and with the promise of support through his psychotherapy we are persuaded to take him.

Amy

Amy knows how to turn in formal academic productions good enough to get by in a non-college curriculum. However, no one interested in Amy was satisfied with what she was doing, and apparently, neither was Amy herself. "She won't grow up and assume responsibility . . . She is restless and nervous . . . Her big trouble is that she is careless . . . She's a dreamer who obviously could do so much more than she does . . . She's willing and compliant, but there is something negative about her . . . She's perfectly capable of doing excellent work, but she never seems to get it done." Amy is sixteen and passing all her courses in the tenth grade with fair marks. She is in psychotherapy, and a change of schools is primarily part of a plan to meet circumstances arising from the progress of her therapy. She is trying to build a new life away from home, and to make a general inquiry about the path of her future development. Her mother is the main force in the family and a highly educated woman, but Amy resents her coldness. We were told that Amy considers school failure an expression of femininity essential in her struggle to become a woman. She is a small, wiry, and neatly formed girl who flirts self-consciously, but can change moods suddenly, becoming unaccountably self-absorbed and almost indifferent to people around her. She talks easily and well, and speaking about her own problems, she seems refreshingly candid. She is also considering application to a nearby preparatory school with high academic standards. We say she does not need our help if she thinks she can handle such a school.

"Well, I think I would do very much better if I can be where the classes are small . . . I think if I didn't feel I had to do it, I could do the work at my own pace in my own way. Then I'd probably do school work. I'd like to make my own program. If I went to preparatory school I'd never last. I get depressed, and then I just can't work until I find out what's bothering me. Can I learn French here? I've always wanted a chance to learn it at my own speed. I need practice in writing compositions . . . I really love math . . . I think you'd understand me and my problems pretty well, and that's what I need. Please give me a chance!"

It is natural for bright and sensitive students to wish for close contact with teacher and informal classrooms. Some will indeed do better under those conditions, but as far as Amy is concerned, we have our doubts. All the same we are going to take her and hope she is right in what she says.

Tom

Tom does not learn at all in school, and we are asked to find out what intellectual capacity he has. He is fourteen and failing in the ninth grade. He does not like to read. A neurologist considers Tom's ambidexterity important evidence of a neurological handicap that may seriously block his learning to read. However, there are other factors. Tom missed a lot of school when his lungs were weakened by a serious attack of bronchial pneumonia. He is never entirely free from respiratory difficulty, and currently he is suffering from the effects of a complex allergic reaction. Nevertheless, his father blames his son's failure upon poor teaching rather than frequent absences. "He was never taught the basic rules of grammar, and when he started French they put him in a class for students who were the best in the grade. They thought he knew French because we had lived in Switzerland. Tom didn't have a chance." His father doubts the boy's intellectual potential, but he wants him to be drilled in what he calls the essentials.

One of Tom's teachers reports, "Tom is conscientious, agreeable, and friendly, big for his age, and too fat. In fact, he's a happy-go-lucky slob." The testing psychologist says, "Tom is average, but he prefers failure to struggle." The educational consultant who referred him declares, "Tom is lacking in drive, passive, and unconcerned with his lack of success. See if you can find out how to motivate him. There's not much to lose in any case. Maybe he has brains. After all, his two sisters have made excellent records at Stanford and Bryn Mawr."

For the interview Tom squeezes between his bulky parents on the sofa. The family becomes a tight, brooding triumvirate, a ponderous mass like a steamroller. Secure for the moment, Tom's wit begins to sparkle, and we wonder why his intelligence is doubted. He may be the world's worst student, but his observations and understanding are unmistakably quick and penetrating. He has a wicked gleam in his eyes, and a sarcastic sense of humor, sometimes brilliant and nearly always funny. It is also true that he is a slob, over six feet of underdeveloped body too generously padded with preadolescent fat. Suddenly, in the midst of a lively discussion his alert expression fades and his eyes droop. Although a trace of a smile seems to sweep across his smooth features, Tom is almost asleep. Tom's father, a doctor, quickly explains that Tom has to take an anti-allergy pill which has the effect of a soporific. Certainly this medicine can account for some of Tom's supposed dullness. But we ask about Switzerland, where Tom was totally free from his allergic reactions and other sickness. There he was tutored privately and intensively; yet the school problems grew worse. Tom's father discounts psychological explanations, for he regards psychology as a pseudoscience. We are taken aback by the rigidity of the family's stand in the face of Tom's severe learning problems. The boy reads and writes badly, and flounders hopelessly in the face of an academic task. He is pathetically impacted and needs help desperately.

Tom's father is quick to rule out new approaches. He seems to be asking for help yet reluctant to support a plan of exploration. Both parents are rather scornful of educators and their systems, doubting the certainty of any knowledge but that gained in the experimental laboratory. We hope to enlist their support and respect for our educational work, for we are attracted by the light in Tom's briefly awakened eye. We take him—with our fingers crossed.

Ned

Ned is a fragile, loose-jointed boy with a cheerful, mobile face. He looks unfinished, as do many fourteen-year-olds with their blunted, slightly swollen features and a kind of boiled look around the mouth and eyes.

Ned has been examined many times by psychologists, doctors,

and teachers, who emphasize separate aspects of his complicated and confused personality. "He's a callow high school kid so spineless that he's incapable of the hard work of learning . . . He speaks up in class; has a superior mind . . . He'd be all right if he had good language training . . . He's so sensitive tears spring to his eyes all the time . . . His fear of failure is the reason for his failure." Ned is fourteen and barely passing his subjects in the ninth grade. He was given intelligence tests almost every year until he reached high school, and the results were nearly always in the superior range. The folder has a record containing comments from all his teachers, beginning with kindergarten, where he was "reserved and high strung." In grade three his reading test scores were low in comparison with the rest of his class, and he then began the tutoring program which eventually led to RSS. In grade four his teacher reported that he was "dependent on adult help." Every year after this the gap between Ned's estimated ability and his achievement test scores grew wider, until at last these scores were running well behind grade level. Tutoring continued, and so did testing. Although in the eighth grade "anxiety is not interfering with Ned's learning," the manila folder says that he read and spelled badly. His tutors now say that his development is at a standstill. Despite close scrutiny by an enlightened school guidance department, Ned's learning failure is a mystery.

Here is a thoroughly worked-over boy, who now looks like a lost cause. What can we do with him when so many excellent teachers and other experts have accomplished so little? In the interview we are attracted by Ned's lively and appealing intelligence. He is a tall, reedy boy with swift and graceful movements. His face is seldom quiet, for he is quick to observe and react. His parents are reeling off his story and Ned enters enthusiastically into the spirit of things when they dwell on his shortcomings. His eyes become moist while the tale unfolds but they dart searchingly about. Why is he not more depressed and discouraged? He is keyed up and alert, and though actively keeping tabs on us, he also seems smugly to believe he is controlling the interview. Asked what he thinks his responsibility for learning it, Ned becomes tough and spiteful, shedding the guise of compliance to reveal a new, intriguing, and hopeful side to his character. We take him.

Franny

Franny is seventeen. She goes to a small private school where she has been finishing last for years. Now she is locked out of their tenth grade, and as she does not qualify for a college-course tenth grade in any other local preparatory school, she and her parents think it is time for remedial measures. The manila folder says she is brighter than any of her intelligence tests show, predicting that if all were well she would test in the superior range. "Franny blows up under pressure of any kind. . . . She could do better, but she works too hard at things. . . . Of course we want her to be happy, but she has to learn how to read faster. . . . She's a good sport and never flinches, even when it hurts. . . . Why can't she throw herself into her work the way her brothers do? . . . She is so careless, she is painfully workable-with," are her teachers' comments.

Franny is a tall, sturdy, open-faced girl, conventionally healthy, conventionally well-dressed, conventionally controlled. She looks like the very model of a good sport and her being out of step in school seems to be her one adventure in bad taste. In our interview a surprising degree of intelligence flashes through her ordinary and regular features, permeating somehow the aggressive correctness of her manner. Franny admits she reads little and without enjoyment. Her parents fuss over reading speed. When her difficulties in school began, she thought the headmaster was sympathetic at first. Then he shifted to scathing criticisms which deeply wounded her feelings. His attitude was inconsistent, and Franny, in self-defense, became intransigeantly unapproachable. Now no one knows what to do.

Franny's mother is an organizer who is going to let the Garden Club drift until she sees to it that her four bouncing children get to all the dentist appointments, doctors' checkups, dancing-school classes, and birthday parties they will ever need. Franny's father is more relaxed and smokes his pipe as if he were taking the ironical view of his wife's tensions. However, when he speaks, he seems to be in full accord with her program. While her mother talks, Franny flushes, but in no other way lets down the guard of her careful manners. Yet inside something must be going wrong, for to us her look betrays anxiety, anger. She expresses indignation about the headmaster's biting remarks to her, and she shows boiling resentment when comparisons are made between her brother and herself. She is sullen when her mother says, "Her father and I have gone along with her on just about everything, but there are some things we have to do even if we don't like them." Tears spring to Franny's eyes when her mother continues, "I have to accept invitations for Franny, or she would never go to parties." Franny holds back no longer: "Stop! Stop! Stop! Must you always manage everything for me?"

Anxious over-nourishment, excessive supervision, and a high-pressured set of expectations cannot entirely seal off this reservoir of feelings. She seems a good bet, and we take her.

Larry

Larry is thirteen, illiterate, and untalkative. Although he has finished the fifth grade he has never completed the requirements of grade two. His teacher says, "Larry is not able to comprehend fourth grade level work. Therefore he is marked U, and advanced to grade five." It is tragic when a public school teacher has no rational alternatives for his over-age students but has to promote them.

One teacher tried to describe Larry's problem, saying, "He blocks completely when the pressure is put on and shrugs his shoulders and is silent." Two major hospitals have examined Larry and characterized his intelligence as bordering on defective. They differed, however, as to diagnosis of his learning failure. One hospital attributed it to brain damage, though they could point to nothing conclusive in the neurological examination. The other, while not discounting brain damage, concluding rather hesitantly that Larry might be suffering from a massive psychological block, and psychotherapy as well as special schooling were recommended. We are asked to do whatever we can to teach Larry reading and simple arithmetic. Larry's stepfather brings him to the interview. Our first reaction is against accepting so strange a boy. He is physically small and underdeveloped, and his whole presence radiates hostility and fear. His spirit is so famished that even his little belly seems distended with hunger. He throws glances at us with glistening, huge, brown eyes that devour everything in range, but he will not meet our gaze. He answers our questions with, "I don't know," keeping his wide eyes down and pulling away like a wounded, wild creature. He shakes with fear, and chokes on the turmoil of powerful feelings that may never find their way out. Larry's father, looking hard-eyed and cynical, is unexpectedly gentle with him, a gentleness which lends a touching quality to their relationship. After the interview, we find ourselves in disagreement because Marilyn says that she feels a physical revulsion at Larry's ferret-like furtiveness, and she will not be able to teach him. I refuse to accept the total responsibility for him and we argue. At last we decide to take Larry because his complex and mysterious problems will test our ideas rigorously. We plan a special program for him. He will have private instruction during school hours, apart but not away from us and the other students. We will closely supervise the work, and bring Larry into the regular program as soon as possible. Our proposal to accept him as a student hinges on the approval of his parents and their agreement to accept the project as experimental.

These nine children never existed. They are nine kinds of adolescents in search of remedial help, emerging from the steam of six years' experience and experiment at RSS. Selection of the real individuals often involved the technical assistance given by diagnostic testing. This was valuable above all when we administered our own mixture of Rorschach, Wechsler-Bellevue Intelligence Scales, and spelling tests in conjunction with assorted standardized achievement tests. Such a battery allowed us to speculate about connections between a student's individually characteristic approach to problem-solving and weak spots in his academic achievements. It might spell out the kind of intelligence he had or the richness of his latent resources; equally it might warn of a proclivity to act out feelings too impulsively for us; in quantifying his qualities, it ranged them on various scales for purposes of comparison with the general population, or a segment of it. However, we could not count on the complete availability of these helpful data, and learned that if we were sufficiently sensitive and experienced, we could pick up information we needed through active, fervid interviewing.

We never literally began a school year with eight rookies as untried as these "types," for admissions were, in fact, spread through the year from August to May. Students accepted in February or later generally returned after the summer vacation. Thus our September starters always included some already on the trip narrated in the chapters ahead.

II ❧ *Reading Is War*

RSS BEGINS WEEKDAY MORNINGS AT 8:30, when I open the front door. If there is an early bird pacing on the porch, he flings me a reproachful look for making him wait. At 8:45 Marilyn arrives, and at 9:00 scheduled classes start for the full-time students. The first, reading, is a combined literature and discussion class in which students take turns reading aloud from a required text. At first we are likely to end up discussing the readers, but our goal is to concentrate on the book and its meanings. At 10:30 we "break" for a twenty-minute period of relaxation and food in the kitchen. The next class is math which runs forty-five minutes, followed by composition for another forty-five. Once in a while a student substitutes an elective subject for math, but generally the morning classes are required "courses." At 12:30 we break again for a period that easily stretches to 1:00. Then begins the last period, one in which the students have more choices. There is a formal class in ancient history for those who want to try learning under a more traditionally subject- and drill-centered discipline. The rest use this hour for independent reading and study. We stay close to this schedule, but all our routines are subject to temporary interruptions and individual adjustments. However, there is no day when full-time students remain at RSS after 2:00 P.M.

Two of our eight are not yet full-time. Larry, whose illiteracy keeps him apart, comes at 9:00 and leaves after the second break. He has a new teacher, Mrs. Hunt, who, except for the breaks, works alone with him in a separate room. Alden, whose two-year absence from school has turned out to be a more serious obstacle than anyone supposed, does not come during the morning, but after 2:00, when I am free to tutor him. With the approach of opening day in September, he suddenly lost his nerve, refusing to have anything at all to do with school. At the last minute, helped by his psychiatrist, he was able to enter a special afternoon tutoring program, aware, of course, that its design was to lead him into full-time work.

This morning Ned is early and gives me a fishy smile that, like Matt's "Sirs," is laid on to give offense. His eyes are bright when he pointedly neglects to greet me to express disappointment at not finding Marilyn there. Probably he genuinely misses her, but I "get" the point and ask him to say "good morning" to me anyway. He claims he already did, bringing to mind that tough quality we thought hopeful when he turned spiteful in the interview. Currently he is speechless with admiration for Jimmy. To him the swagger of Jimmy's defiance is world-challenging. Franny, coming in after Marilyn, looks around for Amy, the only other girl. Franny is still the picture of health and good sense that she was when we first met her, but now she seems more lonely and depressed. She cheers up a little when she spots Marilyn. Amy is not yet here, but she is too unlike Franny to give her much company when she is. Where Amy flirts, Franny looks for camaraderie, treating the boys like friendly brothers. Matt enters just before nine o'clock. His beard has become thick and curly, but his spotted clothes are thinner and more frayed than ever. He is the only student to start off with his own car, an unclean little Renault known as the Vomit 250.

The nettled company gathering around the reading table are generally unable to concentrate on the content of a book, and some are specifically unable to read it well, that is, they have reading blocks. A few are edgy about events at home, but all are harrowed by conflict the moment they get a whiff of school responsibilities. As litmus turns red in the presence of acid, they turn against us as teachers with antagonisms that choke learning. It is quite true that they are getting to like us as persons, just as they like coming to RSS, but the growing ambivalence of their feelings at this stage plunges them the more deeply into trouble. The beginnings of personal attachment will not help them unless they can express and explore their disaffections.

We try to develop these insights in school in direct relation to learning and reading. Literature steeped in the realities of human experience speaks openly to the students about the one human condition that preoccupies them, its weakness, its suffering, its disappointments. This autumn we are reading *Lord of the Flies*, by William Golding. Telling the history of civilization as if it were an account of a group of boys who were marooned while fleeing a nuclear holocaust, this novel touches upon questions close to the serious concerns of our students. It turns upon the conflict between magical and rational answers to primitive fear and ignorance. As the author sees it, and as many adolescents do, this is a conflict between good and evil. As each character epitomizes one striking human quality, it is relatively easy for our students to sympathize with the problems and feelings of at least one of the protagonists.

We are in the large and comfortable living room. Worn easy chairs stand against the walls. We are seated in front of the fireplace around an old-fashioned, oval dining table that has long since resigned itself to dishonor. Amy, later in the year, would describe it in a composition as,

"Quite shaky. The bottom of the table is fairly free from holes and slashes. The sides are mostly holes. The top is so bumpy and rough with all kinds of abrasions. Many hostile feelings have been taken out on this table."

At this moment, Marilyn is talking. "It's a couple of minutes past nine and time to read. Amy's late, but we won't wait for her."

"Where's the other boy you said was coming?" asks Ned accusingly. "You said there would be eight of us."

"Alden? He isn't coming to the group just now. He has some terribly strong feelings against coming regularly to school."

"Who doesn't?" says Jimmy, and everyone laughs.

"Is he some kind of a nut or something that he doesn't come?"

"Oh, come on! Lay off!" I urge. "You all have a fight with school, but your problems are different. Actually Alden comes in the afternoon and I tutor him then. I'm trying to get him to join the group soon, but so far he can't."

"Maybe he'd come if he could go in with Larry and have Mrs. Hunt for his teacher. Man, she's pretty." Tom leers at the closed door leading to the room where Mrs. Hunt and Larry work. Mrs.

Hunt is a young, glamorous, fragile-looking blonde whom the boys all consider beautiful. She is distant, but not shy, and the other students usually have a respect, even admiration for her quietness and reserve.

"Alden's afraid of any regular schedule now," I say. "I don't know him well enough to understand it. I realize you want to see him, and as I said, I hope I can get him at least to visit the class very soon."

"Is that settled? Let's read now. Does everybody have a book?" asks Marilyn.

Of course no one has a copy and Marilyn's question is a signal for a general attack on the books and loose papers piled together in mixed and uneven stacks against a pottery bowl, set like a navel in the center of the table. The students are fascinated by the random play of colored clays in the vase, and they love to feel its smooth roundness. It too inspires mixed feelings, for the students idly scribble Anglo-Saxon commands on the whitish bands, and now as the class begins, they throw cigarette butts and used Kleenex into it. The search for copies of *Lord of the Flies* spreads out the piles of papers and books, and the pottery passes to Matt. The Kleenex box is another cult object with more intricate rites. Marilyn maintains the supply of paper tissue for herself, but all the students dip into it to clean their glasses, wipe their noses and eyes, or mop up spilled coffee, or have something to tear to bits. Perched atop the bookcase, like an idol looking down, is a commemorative grocery carton, whited and decorated to resemble a grotesque tissue box. It bears the inscription, "Pour le nez de Mme. Bernstein," having been presented to her as a symbolic replacement on her birthday last year. The current Kleenex box, like the bowl, becomes the property of one student or another for the entire hour. Ned, who has grabbed it, is now its unofficial Keeper and is already punching holes with his pencil. The hunt for one last copy of our book continues. Ned, seeing a chance to look helpful, leaps up and fumbles about the bookcase, loudly rattling loose papers.

"I can't find any more copies."

"All right, Ned. Sit next to me, and we can share this one. Matt, will you please share yours with Jimmy?"

"Ugh!"

"No!" Jimmy says. "I'll give Matt mine and me and Tom can use one together."

Matt and Jimmy have been enemies from the first. Jimmy's Rotarian conventionality is scandalized by Matt's beard and slovenly dress. Matt's showy interest in culture, his sophisticated language and social pretentiousness bear out Jimmy's claim that Matt lives in "phoneysville" and they belong on opposite sides of the tracks. Jimmy is proud of knowing what a "six-pack" is and he hopes never to hear another word about Dylan Thomas. As tribal enemies they will clash for the rest of the year. Their antagonism may be fed by an incipient mutual attraction, but sparks fly all the same. At the moment we want them to understand that once such feelings can be plainly stated, they need not flare into violence.

"Matt, you really have it in for Jimmy, haven't you?"

"Huh? I don't care for the type very much, if that's what you mean."

"Look at him with his moth-eaten beard! Ask him what he wants to prove. Geeezus! Why doesn't he ever get his jacket cleaned?" Jimmy is stung by Matt's insulting manner.

"You're getting pretty angry, aren't you?" Marilyn says.

"You bet! C'mon. Let's read! That creep makes me too mad."

"All right, everyone? Franny, will you start please? At the bottom of page 88."

The class settles down. Ned, sitting at Marilyn's side, has his eyes dutifully on the book they share, but his hands and energies are devoted to punching a single line of holes as a band around the Kleenex box. Tom and Jimmy are ostentatiously poring over their book, but they twitch and jerk as if kicking at each other under the table. Matt's eyes stare over the top of his book and his lips move in what appears to be a silent count of Ned's holes. The room is not noisy, and Franny begins to read. Her voice is low and she reads haltingly, head bent, hands gripping the book tightly. Her face is flushed, whether from self-consciousness or effort is hard to say. She falters before every word, but seldom pauses for a period. She strings words together with no regard for commas, her phrasing guided neither by syntax nor meaning. Franny is a big, sturdy girl, but she reads like a small child who has been called upon to recite a piece beyond her understanding. Constantly becomes "constantial," and situated is "suited." She even misreads simple words: "sail" for slay, "tired" for tried; and she hesitates over "is." The whole performance is embarrassingly infantile, and the other students fidget.

"What's bothering you, Franny? You're missing words you know, and you don't pay attention to punctuation. Don't you know 'is' or 'tired'?" We stop her because we cannot take these mistakes at their face value. They are like the "I don't know" defense commonly used to answer questions that are considered intrusive. "I don't know" in such cases means "I don't want to say," or "I won't let you put me on the spot." Errors like Franny's proclaim inner negative reactions; to help her find out what they are since she may be afraid of finding out for herself, we must ask.

Franny looks up, shifts nervously in her chair, but does not answer. The others turn to the holes in the table, shred Kleenex, or blacken all the *b*'s and *p*'s on the page. Jimmy stares directly at Franny.

"Franny, why?" I ask.

"It's all right, Franny," says Marilyn. "We're not accusing or scolding you. Mr. Heinemann only wants to find out. You do recognize 'is' and those other simple words, don't you?" Franny's features relax a little as she turns and looks silently at Marilyn. At last she nods.

"OK. Why do you misread them, then?" I ask again. She almost smiles and shrugs her shoulders.

"I don't want to let it go at that, Franny. If you tried to answer the question you might get an idea."

"Why! Why! Why!" exclaims Jimmy. "It's like a dentist's drill. Do you have to get in there?"

"I think I do."

"I know why you misread, Franny," says Marilyn. "It's because you're thinking about something else."

"Right," I say, "and I'm trying to persuade you to say what it is."

"Don't you want to tell us, Franny?"

The silence thickens, and her eyes shine with tears, but her lips purse into a firm line.

"I want to help, not criticize, but how can I if you don't tell me what's wrong?"

The noise of Tom's pen digging into the table is the only sound.

Suddenly Franny explodes, "You always try to get me to say I'm angry or something's on my mind."

"Isn't that true?"

"Well, there is after you put it there," she replies sullenly. "It's your idea, not mine."

"You're upset now, Franny. Why do I make you so angry?"

She shrugs her shoulders again, and looks down.

"Tell him, Franny," interjects Ned. "This is beginning to get good. Go on, tell him off."

"He'd have a cow," Franny murmurs.

"No, he wouldn't. He wants you to speak up," says Marilyn.

"Well, you take everything so seriously here. Things aren't all that bad. I make reading mistakes because I'm careless."

This dissent is a small breakthrough for Franny and now her eyes are dry.

"Who told you you were careless?"

"Everybody." She laughs.

"Why are you careless about reading?"

"I'm not when I read to myself. I don't like to read aloud."

"Have you done it a lot?"

"Yes. I've always had trouble with my reading. My mother used to say that there was something wrong with my eyes, and I had to do a million eye exercises. But I never thought it was my eyes. Anyway, the headmaster in my last school taught my English classes and made me read out loud. He yelled at me every time I made any mistake. You had to be perfect for him!"

"You poor kid! No wonder you don't like to read out loud."

"What you mean is, she's furious, don't you? I'll bet she got really burned when her teacher was so mean to her," puts in Ned.

Franny's eyes fill again, and she blushes deeply. If she is angry, she is also miserable.

"Franny, I'm sorry you feel so bad, but we now realize how much reading out loud distresses you. Maybe the reasons go deeper, too. If you get too embarrassed to read again, I hope you'll say so instead of just suffering through it. Perhaps then we can talk more about your feelings. Matt, will you read next, please?"

"Uh! Where are you?"

Our concentration on Franny has left Matt cold. He has been ostentatiously leafing through to the end of *Lord of the Flies* as if he could not wait until he found out what happened. Now he looks up and gazes balefully around the room, wiping his glasses with a tissue, in a vigorous and purposeful motion wholly at variance with his casual appearance. Bearded, still sockless and unpressed, he slumps in his chair, his handsome and expressive face disdainful. He seems to think he has dropped into a lesser world here where his sensitivity and intellectuality raise him high above us. Where is the seriousness we observed in our interview? He is fumbling with his book and giggles insolently.

"I get the message, Matt. When you say, 'Where are you?' you want us to see that you don't consider yourself part of this class," I say.

"Brilliant deduction, sir! Just what you would say, sir! I have my own analysis, but you'd only ruin it with your interpretations. Can't we just read?"

"OK. Good. Page 89."

Matt begins. He is a good, theatrical reader whose voice is expressive even when he is not in a good mood. His ability to project moods and ideas annoys yet fascinates the others. Now, he is reading well, and they are following in the text when Amy quietly slips in the front door, removes her coat, and takes a seat at the table. Matt looks up from his book, and stops reading. Amy, a fragile blonde, looks haggard and unwashed. Her hair dangles down in a stringy tangle. She seems exhausted and old.

"For God's sake, Amy! What happened to you? Have you been up all night?"

"Oh, no. As a matter of fact I overslept. That's why I'm late. Sorry."

"Why do you look so awful?" demands Matt.

"Oh, do I? What's the matter with me?"

"You forgot to wash your face and comb your hair," says Marilyn.

"Hmmm. Did I? I guess I did. Well, I was upset this morning."

"You're late, too."

"Well, I guess I am."

"Why?"

"Do we have to go into that?" asks Jimmy. "I thought this was a reading class. But all we do is get started and then talk about something else."

"Why were you and Tom snickering, then?"

"Well, she looks as if she'd been having a night of it," Tom giggles.

"She's disgusting," exclaims Jimmy. "Don't richies have bath-tubs?"

"Bourgeois bastard," answers Matt.

"You———"

"That'll have to wait, boys. We are trying to settle why Amy is late."

"Yes, Amy. You said you were upset."

"Well, I had a fight with my father last night. I thought he'd apologize this morning. But he didn't."

This sets Tom and Ned off. They exchange knowing, skeptical glances, probably amusing themselves with fantasies about orgies. Franny, carefully groomed and dressed in richly sensible clothes, does not allow herself a rude comment, but seems to share Jimmy's revulsion against the Unclean. Amy is too self-absorbed to notice these reactions.

"Tom and Ned! Do you want to add any comments of your own? You look as if you had some," I say.

"No."

"Amy," says Marilyn, "you must get here before nine. We can't let you break that rule. Even if you are upset. Now I'm going to say that you have to be here by a quarter to nine. And no ex-cuses."

"But this is the first time I've been late in weeks."

"No, Amy. I've got it in the book. Want to see it? Twice last week. And all the other days you get here just on the dot. Like a little child balancing on a rail to show off. You've fallen too often."

Getting to school on time is an unpretentious, and often hard-fought achievement in self-reliance. This early step toward meeting more complex learning schedules is difficult for some even when we stand firm against their alibis.

"OK. Amy, will you please go and fix yourself up now?"

"All right. I will, if that's what you want me to do."

Amy leaves and Matt prepares to resume reading. The others continue to be restless. In a moment or two Amy returns. She has only pushed the hair out of her face, but Marilyn thinks we have made enough of this point. We go back to our book.

This incident with Amy is one of many—like those moments of almost total indifference to others which puzzled us in our interview. We are still far from understanding it.

"Amy, I hope you have the book with you. One is missing and we had to double up before you came."

Amy rummages about in her green baize bag and pulls out two copies. She takes books home every night, although she never uses them. Larry and Jimmy do the same. Indeed, after a long day of resistance to school work, all three pack and carry off a load of textbooks and notebooks. Next morning they lug them back to school unopened. They become book carriers because they want to take something away from school. Some stuff their bags to create an impression of being regular, the outward sign to the world that they are really going to school.

"Amy, why did you take two copies home? We really needed one of them."

"I don't know. It must have been a mistake. I wasn't sure which copy was mine, and I had to leave in a hurry yesterday."

"The copies are all the same, and they belong to the school. What difference does it make which one you have?"

"I like my copy, and that's the only one I want to use. I don't want anyone else to have it."

"All right. But don't take home more than one again! As a matter of fact, you aren't the only one who is taking home the book and not reading it. I wish everyone would leave them here! Then they'd be here when we need them."

"Jeez! I've heard everything. What would my old man say if he heard you? You're telling us not to take books home!"

"For Christ's sake!" Matt exclaims sullenly. "If you want me to read, why can't you all be quiet? Amy's a wreck this morning. I hate it when she takes up so much time. I want to get on with the book."

Ned snickers. He has long ago laid aside his book; absorbed in himself, he shreds the Kleenex box. Jimmy leans back in his chair; balanced on its hind legs, he clutches the top of the mantelpiece, but too late. He plummets out of sight, crashing to the floor. Hoots of laughter die out as he rises again chastened and blushing.

"Are you hurt?"

"No, I'm all right. I just feel silly."

"Think nothing of it—as long as you're not hurt. Somebody does it every year."

"He only did it because I said I wanted to read," says Matt.

"I doubt it, Matt," says Marilyn. "I doubt if he believes any more than I do that you are really interested in this story. You never know where the place is. Maybe you do hate to have Amy's problems take up our attention, but she came in looking miserable and feeling worse, and we had to try to give her a hand."

"Give her a hand! It sounded more like giving her the business," says Jimmy. "Not that I object."

"Be fair, Jimmy, we had to tell her to pull herself together. I hope she can work now."

"Besides," I add, "think of the times when you've come in so low that we've had to drop everything for you. We do that with everyone."

"Let's read now," says Marilyn.

With help, Matt again finds his place and begins to read. There are noisy adjustments at the table as each student, in his own good time, picks a book and finds the place. Ned stops torturing the box, and we begin to feel that at last we can get on with the work. Matt's reading becomes dramatic as the struggle in the novel between two antithetical characters, Ralph and Jack, reaches a sharp climax. At stake is the leadership for survival of a whole group of marooned boys, but the conflict is more than the outcome of personal strivings. Ralph is a steady, easy-going, and essentially reasonable boy who naturally became the first leader. Jack is a nervous, angry, and authoritarian fellow who needs followers, and asserts his masculinity by becoming a hunter. In this way he replaces Ralph as leader. The students seem to be fascinated by the boys and the issues between them. When Matt reads in his tense voice, "The two boys faced each other. There was the brilliant world of hunting, tactics, fierce exhilaration, skill; and there was the world of longing and baffled common sense," the group is tuned in, following closely. Questions and comments pour from students and flow into conversation and discussion. Each tries to identify himself or another with one of the leading characters, and each picks someone in the book to defend. Only Franny remains silent. Jimmy comes to life briefly when Tom mentions how much he longs for his own tropical island where he could watch television dramas and movies all day without having anyone nag him. The discussion of escape and breadfruit appeals to all of them. Jimmy's dreamland is a similar island where he would sling a hammock, and lie with a pile of sandwiches within easy reach on one side and racks of Cokes on the other. Apparently he would be alone. In the near distance his private drag strip would gleam in the sun. Everyone laughs sympathetically and we feel quiet satisfaction. After a ragged beginning it now looks as if we have dealt with the most urgent problems.

To achieve this peaceful and productive moment we have been cautiously threading our way over a battleground, neither provoking nor sidestepping collisions. Now, listening to a story, reading it, moving in with its characters, the students are passing into a new world where thinking, feeling, and learning are one. Later in the year this experience comes more easily and more often; now it is an interlude between wars.

It is Jimmy's turn to read, and he raises no objections. He seldom makes mistakes, but his voice is monotonous and he reads too fast. A tight quaver in his voice shows he is unwilling. The class follows intently while he reads half a page. Suddenly a loud, jarring bell rings out. Amy jumps, Tom curses, Ned giggles, and Matt rolls his eyes. The aura of good will has blown up.

"Oh God, what's up now?" I demand, startled.

No one answers, but all eyes swivel toward Tom.

"Well, who did it? And what was it?"

Silence.

"Now come on. Whatever it was it wrecked the reading. I want to find out what it was."

"Did you do it, Tom?"

"No . . . I . . ."

"I'll bet he did."

"So will I. Did you, Tom?"

"No."

"Are you sure?"

"Wait a minute," says Jimmy, coloring deeply. "Don't go after him. It was me." He opens his hand showing the pocket watch with an alarm that Tom had brought in and proudly shown around school before class.

"I don't understand you, Jimmy. Why did you break up your own reading?"

"I didn't do it on purpose. It was an accident."

"An accident?" asks Marilyn. "I don't think so. I know you didn't want to read."

"Of course it was," insists Jimmy. "I asked to look at the watch and Tom let me have it. I was wondering what the two knobs were for and I pulled this one out when my turn came. I forgot about the knob. It was a perfect accident."

"Are you really as innocent as you say, Jimmy? Are you sure you weren't secretly hoping the watch would ring just to make someone jump?" I say.

"Boy, you're as bad as Mrs. B. Of course not! It was an accident, that's all!"

Everyone laughs. Amy says disgustedly, "Oh, come on! Let's read! I was just getting interested."

Jimmy concurs with mock seriousness. "Yeah, that's what I say. Let's get on with it."

Marilyn looks steadily at Jimmy. "I don't believe it, Jimmy. I think you wanted to break up the class."

"The timing was perfect," Matt mutters audibly.

"Thanks for the pun, Matt. But it's no joke. It was hard work getting settled down this morning, and just when it looked as if we could really have a good class, it goes up in smoke with a loud noise. I'm really disappointed, and I want to find out why Jimmy did it."

"What is there to find out? It was an accident, wasn't it?"

"*I* don't think so."

Jimmy pushes the watch back to Tom, who places it on the table face up before him. He and Tom take up their books and assume the reading "posture" of past schooling. He is too defiant, now, to talk any more.

"I really want to read the story now," Ned speaks up.

It should please us that he wants to take the initiative, but we have already noticed that his moves are stiff and contrived, and now hardness flashes in his eyes. Is he on "our" side or is he counting on Tom and Jimmy to divert us from reading? Does he know that there is so much unresolved tension in the class that continued reading is out of the question anyway? He may dread that a complete discussion of the "accident" will lead to a clearing of the air and a return to academic work. Ned rarely starts trouble, but he takes advantage of incidents to prevent serious discussion. While his smile is ready and his eyes bright and intelligent, every expression has an elusive quality and his cooperation always has something oblique about it.

"It's Amy's turn, but if you are eager to read, Ned, you can take her place."

"I wouldn't want to push ahead of anyone. Age before beauty, anyway. I'll wait for my turn."

"Sweet child isn't he? A real infant," Amy cracks back.

"All right, Amy, will you start again please?"

"Well, could you tell me just where we were? Was it page 87?"

"No. We finished page 87 yesterday. We're at the bottom of page 89. You had me fooled. I thought you were interested in the story, but you haven't been following it at all."

"I'm interested now."

"What about before?"

"I'll admit I wasn't with it. I mean my mind was on something else. Anyway, how can you expect me to remember anything after that blasted alarm went off? There was too much tension and talk."

"Did you think it was a perfect accident?"

"No. I certainly didn't. I think Jimmy wanted to start something because he was angry."

"I wish you had said that when we were talking about it. Instead you pretended you wanted to read."

"That's true, I was faking it. But I didn't want to go into it. Why should Jimmy get to be the center of attention that way?"

"But you didn't really want to read when you said you did. You lost the place because you didn't care where it was."

"I guess you could put it that way."

"If you had said you didn't want Jimmy to be the center of attraction at the time you felt it, we would have discussed why he got the limelight and why you felt so competitive."

"I'd rather not talk about that now."

"Well, all right. But the point is that if you said what your true feelings were, in the end we'd get more work done."

"I get it. You don't have to beat me over the head with it."

"That's how a teacher can get nowhere with you. As soon as I act teachery you get angry. Still, you don't have to read now if you're too preoccupied. Ned has said he would. Please, Ned. Let's try once more."

"OK. Where Simon is looking for Piggy's 'specs'?"

"Yes."

Ned is a poor reader by any standards. He reads too fast, running words together and giving the impression that he relies on speed to draw attention away from his mistakes. He substitutes his own words for the author's, "around" for "about," and impatiently alters verb endings, "crouches" for "crouching." He omits most three-letter words regardless of meaning. When he reads more slowly many mistakes vanish, but his usual attack is compulsively swift and careless. If we slow him down, his speed accelerates as soon as he loses track of our pressure. His mistakes flaunt a lack of interest in content, and we can no longer restrain ourselves.

"Ned, what kind of reading is that? Those are easy words and you skip over them or misread them at will. What's the matter?"

"I don't know. That's the way I read."

"I know that. But it's pretty bad."

"Can I smoke while you're talking, Mr. Heinemann?" interrupts Matt.

"No, Matt. Not during class time. By the way, do you have your parents' permission to smoke?"

"My parents don't care if I smoke or not. I should think you'd let us smoke in these small classes. Why can't we?"

"There is a fire hazard but mainly because you wouldn't be allowed to smoke in a regular classroom. It's a realistic rule we keep during class. Now, Ned, about your reading. Will you try to read better?"

"I can't."

"You always read better when you slow down."

"He won't slow down because he isn't following the story anyway."

"I'm interested, but I've read enough. It's someone else's turn. I'll gladly move out of the spotlight."

"Tom, will you read now?"

"I'm dying for a smoke, Mr. Heinemann. Can't I please?"

"You can go outside and smoke on the porch, Matt. Not in here."

"Go ahead, Tom. Read."

Matt is undecided, annoyed, but not smoking. He does not want the inconvenience of going outside, nor can he concentrate on reading. Tom begins to read, but giggles uncontrollably as he plows along. He too reads badly, but does not pretend to make a serious effort. No one listens and each sinks more deeply into his preoccupations. There is no point in keeping up a pretense of an organized class now, but before we can decide to make Tom stop, the air again rings with the alarm. Amy jumps a second time, but the whole class looks pleased and Tom bursts into gales of laughter.

"That time you really did it, Tom, didn't you?"

"Yup."

"It's just as well. What reading! And what a class! Everyone is in a state!" says Marilyn.

"Well, why did you, Tom?" I ask.

"For a joke."

"Laugh away. But it's no joke. How mean can you kids be? You've defeated every move we've made to get somewhere in the book this morning."

"Aw, don't take it so seriously. A joke's a joke."

Troubled students often retreat into attempts at humor, asking us to laugh good-naturedly at their clowning and conspire with them to trifle with a world that defeats them. If they would follow the narrative of the *Lord of the Flies* they might get a better grip on their problems. Our failure to get our group to focus on the book is bitterly disappointing. However, if we can lead them to realize that they are even more thwarted by their own doing, then all may benefit from this episode.

Turning to Tom I say, "Whatever made you think anything funny was going on?"

"Well, didn't everyone laugh?"

"Neither Mrs. B nor I did. How can we laugh? We haven't made any progress this morning. Your comic mood is false. You're upset—not happy. Tense—not relaxed. Restless—not satisfied. We can't laugh when we know your feelings underneath are a misery to you."

"I haven't made a secret about my feelings," pouts Amy. "I've already told you I was upset over an argument with my father. I'm still nervous because I expected him to call me here and apologize for what he said. He hasn't called, though."

"What was the argument about?"

"Well, it's really something I'm working on in my therapy. I don't know whether I should tell you about it. Anyway, I won't say it in front of the whole group."

"If you think talking about it will make you feel better and free you to do schoolwork, we can go into the front room and talk privately."

"Never mind! Not now."

When a student is thinking about matters unrelated to school, he may need to speak about them before he can work. Taking it up privately saves time for him, while the rest of the class suffers less from irrelevant discussion. In the present case, Amy's problems may have nothing to do with the schoolwork, although she uses her genuine anxiety to justify her behavior. We leave our offer open, wishing now to inquire further into Tom's action.

"Well, Tom? Back to you and the watch!"

"Why can't anyone make a joke around here? If I make a joke you say I'm angry. That's ridiculous!"

"Did you set the watch off on purpose?"

"Oh, yes."

"You knew it would break up the reading class."

"Of course I did."

"How is that funny?"

"Anything that gets you going is funny. You rush to the panic button right away. You take everything so seriously! Besides, I thought that you were bad when you blamed Jimmy for something that was an accident. I really didn't want to break up the class, though."

"So, Tom. You didn't really want us to laugh at a joke and you're sorry you broke up the class besides. We were right to take it seriously."

"I know what's got him," says Jimmy. Having won Tom's loyalty and support, he takes a sharp pleasure in pinning him down to watch him squirm. "You accused me of plotting when it was an accident, and he did the same thing as I did, the dumb jerk, just to get even with you."

Despite Jimmy's cruelty Tom grins and nods in agreement. Although he does nothing to change himself, Tom is ashamed of his own awkward fat, and feels physically inferior to Jimmy at a time of life when physical development is transcendingly important. Jimmy senses and takes advantage of this. Matt is outraged by Jimmy's heartless domination of Tom, and he bursts out:

"My God! This is a mess!"

"Are you on Tom's side, Matt?"

"I couldn't care less."

"What do you mean by a 'mess'?"

"Oh, the whole thing. What am I doing with all these kids? I don't belong here."

"Thanks, pal. Thanks a bunch," says Jimmy.

"We knew you felt that coming here lowered you socially, but you decided to come anyway, didn't you? You have school problems and so have the others. That's the common denominator," I say.

"Is that your sermon for me? I knew I shouldn't have come this morning. I had to force myself, and even when I stood at the door, I knew I didn't want to come in."

"That's spreading it with a trowel—but at least you're saying part of your feelings. What you're not saying is that you came in because you also wanted to."

Matt giggles in disdain.

"OK, Matt. Be a louse. But you know perfectly well you can get up and leave this moment if you want to. No one is forcing you to stay. Do you want to go?"

Matt doesn't answer, but a sullen expression replaces his giggle, and his tension mounts. Perhaps if we had not suggested that he leave, he would feel free to go, though he has never before walked out when angry. Again he cannot choose to do what he wants partly because he's not sure what he wants, and partly because he's afraid. He sulks, but not all his feelings are negative. He has a sense of relief that no disaster strikes when he begins to voice a few of his real thoughts. We turn to Ned, hoping that he, too, may tell us what is on his mind.

"Ned, the only thing we've heard from you this morning is some awful reading, and no explanation."

"Why are you picking on me? I didn't do anything."

"That's right. You didn't. You've given no opinions and you've held yourself aloof from our discussions. How about a contribution?"

"What do you mean?"

"I mean you have to say why you were reading so badly this morning."

"You won't get mad?"

"Probably not, if you tell the truth."

"What else would I tell?"

"Come on!"

"Well, it's the book."

"What's wrong with the book?"

"It's too hard for me. Just too hard."

"You've said all that before. About almost any assignment. I know you don't *like* doing something you think is too hard, but in this case you're wrong. This book is not at all too hard for you. The vocabulary is certainly simple. I think it's easy."

"For you, maybe, but it's not my fault if I can't do it."

The tears well up in Ned's eyes. The tears are real, and we know he feels bad. We would like to challenge him further; yet until we know him better, we dare not. His weeping forces us for the moment to share his helplessness.

We have almost convinced the students that they can openly treat RSS as a battlefield. We want them to read, but they cannot while preparing for war. If only Jimmy will reveal what lay behind the watch ringing, we will be able to show them that it is safe to discuss their warlike impulses.

"Well, Jimmy. How about it?"

"How about what?"

"Your bell ringing broke up the class, whether intentionally or not. I happen to think you meant to do it, and I want to know why."

"Geeesus! Here we go again. Are you some kind of jackhammer or something?"

"I don't care what name you give it. The thing is that it's your problem I'm trying to help you solve. You hurt yourself when you don't allow the class to go on."

"I don't think so. You're sore because you couldn't get us to read."

"Well, a little, though sore's not the right word. No, I think you broke up the class because of some feeling you had, and I want you to talk about it. That's the sort of thing that must have happened in regular school plenty of times."

"You mean you're not going to give me the business—even if it wasn't an accident?"

"No. We want to discuss what it means. You aren't the only one to disrupt the class today, after all."

"No, Amy and Matt have sure caused trouble."

"Well, let's get back to you. Shall I tell you what I think?"

"Yeah!"

"I think you knew there was plenty of discomfort in the class and you wanted to play it up to show your control over us."

"Do you mean I was trying to get everyone to do what I want?" he grins delightedly.

"Yes."

"So tell us why, Jimmy."

"Why?"

"How do you know it wasn't an accident like I said?"

"I don't know. I'm just figuring."

"Well, I'll admit I've broken up plenty of classes at my old school. They always threw me out of class."

"Well, we won't. I'll tell you how I know, Jimmy," I say. "You were fooling around with the watch when you should have been following the story."

"I guess I ought to admit it. You're right. It was no accident. I wanted to break up the class, but not because of the book. I really like it. It was when you kept stopping to discuss things. You asked questions and got everyone to talk about the story. I just got sore."

Jimmy talks fast and to the point. Behind his being "sore" about the birth of a discussion is his feeling that the classroom is a battlefield. His anger seems to him reason enough to destroy the class. Amy's late and bedraggled appearance, Franny's inept stumbling, Matt's scornful isolation, the many distractions that erupted from all sides formed a barricade which excluded them all from *Lord of the Flies*.

We could suppress, ignore, or ride roughshod over their defenses without denting their rigid attitudes or opening their minds to ideas. Were we to soothe or try to persuade them that their worries are really not as important as schoolwork, they would remain unconvinced. We have learned that the only way to grapple with warlike disruption is to foster free discussion of immediate issues. Gradually we develop a clear statement and interpretation of the feelings which provoked the trouble. In the beginning this process does not reduce the incidence of class sabotage. Disruptions may be even more frequent. It is difficult, for students fear the unknown consequences of unpleasant truths. To be taken seriously by adults is for many a new and puzzling experience. However, in the initial stage they learn that wherever truth may lead, it does not bring punishment in school. It is difficult for a teacher to allow his desire to instruct to be diverted into behavioral inquiries. He is forced to "read" the unwilling student's behavior instead of the book. With experience he can guess at the tangle of conflicting impulses and longings that students conceal and to lead them fruitfully out into the open. Teachers and students can agree to a state of war where a challenge is not catastrophic.

III ❧ Larry and Alden

LARRY AND ALDEN will join the full-time group as soon as they are ready. Alden, resistant and skittish, is still steaming away in afternoon tutoring sessions with me. Larry cannot belong to the group until Mrs. Hunt teaches him to read.

Like the others, Larry is depressed and angry. Because his school life has been a continuing disaster unrelieved by a single academic achievement, his bad feelings seem to have been initially byproducts rather than causes of failure. Probes into motivation look like a waste of time where an effective technical approach seems so urgently needed. The possibility of neurological defects and the need to get started suggest traditional remedial measures. But for his unsmiling taciturnity, Larry might be like the youngster pictured in the following conventional presentation of "New" auditory methods:

> The pupil sits before you looking intently at some common word such as "where," or "once," or "said," but is quite unable to recognize it and read it. Not wishing to prolong his suffering you finally pronounce the word, and, perhaps, use it in a sentence. . . . His face lights up as he exclaims, "Oh, is that what the word is? I know that." . . . For example, . . . no amount of looking at the word "once" will result in his knowing it and, therefore, getting meaning from it. Upon hearing the word said, however, the pupil immediately recognizes it and understands its meaning since it is a word that he has used in his own speech for a long time.*

Granted that, as we see it, the light in that eager little face is

---

* Wilson, Rosemary G., and Lindsay, Helen G., "Applying Linguistics to Remedial Reading," *The Reading Teacher*, Vol. 16, No. 6, May 1963. Page 452.

not "discovery" but the flush of victory upon making the teacher do what he ought to do himself, still it appears that the student must be given this unimaginative sort of beginning. When he succeeds with a few words, there is a good chance that he will become less depressed and angry. Larry, too shrunken, too frightened, and too inarticulate to find out what we mean by the interpretation of behavior, offers Mrs. Hunt a green light for methodological experimentation.

We think he wants to come to school, and he hints that he likes us. But the dogged regularity of his attendance is possibly enforced by that cold, tough young man who drives him. Larry thinks of this incongruous companion as his father's business assistant. Having spent his first years amidst Boston's worst slums, Larry's loosely organized family suddenly picked up and moved to a small farm in an outlying and very quiet suburb. Secrecy cloaks this change, and though his background suggests a lurid, even sensational story, speculation would lead us away from the task of teaching him.

Larry has relaxed enough to mutter a greeting when he enters, but his head drops low and he shuffles off dispiritedly to his classroom. We thought him too retarded to want to be in the group reading. We made other mistakes. We decided he needed individual attention from a dedicated, gentle tutor who would immediately sympathize with the tragic misfiring of his early life, a tutor who would combine patience and firmness, to lead Larry through the first steps of learning to read with repetitive drill in phonics and simple, one-syllable words. Both Marilyn and I dislike this work as mindless and boring, but we can help Mrs. Hunt with what is considered baggage essential for any remedial teacher. Marilyn still dislikes Larry, and I am too busy to devote any large block of time to him.

Mrs. Hunt is a graduate of a liberal arts college and used to be an editorial assistant in a publishing firm. There she developed her interest in the way people express themselves as well as in what they say. However, her work with Larry is her first teaching assignment. She has no college credits in remedial teaching or any other educational course. We like her the better for that, as she has escaped being formally indoctrinated with the idea of making games out of detested school work so students can learn without realizing it. Our principles run the other way in horror of the deception. RSS students are too intelligent to be "fooled" into education. Indeed, their disenchantment with learning began or was confirmed when their teachers relied too much on manipulation and indirect controls. Their refusal to be duped is, in our eyes, their best asset, proof of an integrity upon which we intend to build. Teachers, walking into—not around—school hatreds, help defiant students make self-awareness the touchstone to a positive motivation.

Mrs. Hunt is quick about acquiring skills in the methods we think she will need for Larry. She believes she can "come up" with the right responses to his needs as long as honesty prevails. Yet, she is not as outspoken as Marilyn or I. Indeed, she becomes thoughtful and rather aloof when her principles of social tact collide with our brash speaking out the truth and working upon the feelings it arouses. Her own need for restraint and privacy gives her a cool, patient air which, being natural, attracts and holds the quieter, gentler, and more withdrawn students. She is a great favorite with all the boys who think anyway she is a real "babe." This does not register much, though, with Larry.

Pretty teachers may charm or upset young boys. Mrs. Hunt has had neither effect on Larry, whose feelings are still too undifferentiated to be influenced by her beauty. He is not indifferent to her as a person, for he frequently shows her pictures of his family and the farm animals, telling her many simple stories about life at home. All the same, his dullness does not lift, even though his talks with Mrs. Hunt indicate a tentative and groping relationship. She relies on these discussions when he makes especially heavy weather of her efforts to teach him. But if Larry is more at home with us and if he has some kind of an attachment to Mrs. Hunt, he still can't read.

Mrs. Hunt's concern for his lack of progress is growing and she is disappointed by her failure to make the personal relationship influence his ability to learn; but above all she worries about her own reactions. Her sympathy for him does not prevent her becoming increasingly short-tempered, and regrets do nothing to diminish her anger. Despite weeks of work with Larry the simplest syllables are still unlearned and she begins to think him hopeless, for even mastery of a vowel sound is only temporary. Does he really understand there are differences among them? He enunciates so poorly that it is hard to hear what he says. In any case he retains little if anything from one day to the next, and Mrs. Hunt is beside herself. Yet, he is diligent, and he struggles for the upper hand over the stubborn and elusive sounds in the phonics books. She knows that he wants to read, but as time passes, the tension between them becomes grotesque. She pleads with him to tell her what is wrong, but he only reiterates stonily, "I don't get it," and the door that stands ajar slams shut. Mrs. Hunt observes that his resistance to learning grows stronger in direct proportion to the energy she puts into teaching him. Though he stolidly makes great efforts, she feels a contradictory, overpoweringly willful, and furious refusal to learn. She flares up against him so frequently she at last asks to be relieved.

We are pleased with her accomplishment. Though she has failed to teach him, she has somehow kept him coming regularly and she has unquestionably provided a climate in which he may still flourish. But she misunderstands the meaning of his learning block. She takes it as her failure instead of his, because like many other beginning teachers she regards her student's achievement as a measure of her ability. None of us escapes a sense of personal failure when, after our best efforts, there is no measurable growth. This vulnerability becomes especially acute when we try to rescue students from chronic failure; we feel too responsible for them, inadvertently sharing their illusions about our powers. When we started our work we used to suppose some aspect of our personalities could win a change or some new teaching method could induce it in behavior patterns which we knew to be deeply ingrained. When we did not succeed, we felt a terrible challenge to our competence. Made to feel inadequate for our work, we smarted as does Mrs. Hunt when the person we strained to accept, understand, and mold, rejected us. Until the limits of our responsibility became plain, we often struck back in anger at the student whose defiant refusals seemed to prove we could not teach. However, experience has proven that when a student does not intend to learn, no one can teach him; when he wants to defeat the teacher, nothing is easier. Under these circumstances the responsibility of the student himself must be soberly weighed before a teacher disqualifies herself.

Mrs. Hunt's defeat is inevitable because Larry cannot talk about his feelings and she cannot brook his dumb and disobedient rejection of herself. If she knew that neither sympathy nor pedagogical virtuosity helps when a student's mind closes up, as Larry's does, the moment he enters a classroom, she could better control her feelings.

Marilyn and I are baffled because his resistance does not lessen, though his worst fears about us seem to have subsided. We begin to doubt his capacity to learn, and turn for advice to his doctor, a psychoanalyst who has been seeing Larry once a week since the start of school. The doctor has no new evidence to support his faith in the boy's potential, but he is convinced that anger must be the source of the block, not a brain injury or defective intelligence. He urges us to continue our work. Marilyn is sure she cannot work with Larry because of her continuing antipathy. Teachers may try to check their negative reactions to students, but hiding their feelings seldom fools those students who suspect teachers are personally against them anyway. Neither can a teacher who shows too much hostility teach them successfully. The responsibility for Larry is left to me. Fortunately a student's personality seldom antagonizes all teachers at once, and I am certainly more interested in Larry anyway. He is more friendly to me, as are most of our boys who express their hostility with especial force against women teachers and find it relatively easy to form simple relationships with men.

I plan to take Larry in the reading period. This requires some juggling of our schedule. Marilyn has to cope with the full reading class aided only by Mrs. Hunt, more as an observer, than an active helper. It is a strenuous assignment for Marilyn, but by now the students are more at ease and less belligerent. They are still reading *Lord of the Flies* and interest grows in the social war on the island.

It seems to me that Larry is more trouble than the whole reading class in the next room. No magical change occurs because of me. I find, as Mrs. Hunt did, that he does not, will not, or cannot learn, although I know it is not my fault. I give him the word "cat" to read, and I work with him over Dr. Seuss's *Cat in the Hat*—again and again, without the slightest change. He still cannot or will not or just does not learn "cat." He seems to be trying hard. His head bends over his papers. His lips move tantalizingly. At first no sound comes out; sweat forms on his brow; at last the tortured vowel comes. The wrong one! We do it again. Still wrong! He never remembers the sound of a letter for more than a minute or two. We do not give up, though our room sounds like a barnyard, with Larry grunting and groaning out vowels and syllables. He gets angry and so do I, each answering the other's irritation with more anger.

I haul myself in. After all, it is still *his* failure, not mine. Maybe he simply cannot learn. Maybe he is suffering from brain damage; in that case my pressure is cruelly outrageous. I do not know about him, but I know about myself. I have no choice but to deal with him as potentially able to learn. I will try new methods, but there are no games or new ideas for a soul so dismal and joyless. Whatever I do, at the end of a quarter hour Larry murmurs in a voice coated with hate, "I don't get it." Does it help when I restrain my own anger? His blossoms and spreads anyway, and the more I teach the more tense he is. Whether or not I am in a good mood, whether or not he has a brain injury, his fury is an irreducible fact. How can I handle his emotion when he himself cannot articulate it? He has not yet learned to think in any sort of coherent, conceptual way, and in that sense he is not rational. Meanwhile he struggles with himself, returning to these gruesome sessions day after day. In a circle of its own, his own efforts seem to build even higher the blocks that inhibit his learning! He is paralyzing himself in a complex move at once willful and involuntary.

Understanding better the rigid system that chokes Larry's ability to act independently, I remember how I had broken a similar deadlock a few years ago. We had a brilliant eight-year-old named Ben who also had not learned to read. He resisted all teaching and remained an enigma until one day when cornered, he exclaimed, "I will *not* learn to read." My reply was untutored and spontaneous. I said, "If you will not read right now, I will take you across my knee and spank you." Ben stared at me incredulously.

Suddenly he decided that I meant it, and turned to his book. For the first time in his life he began to read. My threat had been enough at first, but the moment came when he had to see whether I could carry it through. I spanked him several times, and he understood that I wanted only to break some internal deadlock that immobilized him, making decisions impossible. He learned to read quickly and we became good friends. Years later his parents reported that reading was what he liked most to do in school.

If Larry's mind could think it, would he say, as Ben did, "I won't learn?" I think so. Anyway, it is something untried, and a method seldom if ever used by remedial teachers. With Larry, I take a firmer stand, explaining every so often that I believe he is refusing to learn. I cite one instance after another to prove that only a determined will could prevent him from reading "cat" correctly. He seems unimpressed, and makes no changes. I threaten him with a slap if he continues to refuse, hoping that he may take the threat for the act, and yield. He does not. It is I who am in the corner, and I have to put up or shut up. One day his "I don't get it" seems more sullen than ever. I strike him. He recoils like a steel spring, shrinking away and then freezing into a crouch while murder spills from eyes fixed unblinkingly on me. He wants to claw me apart.

For a moment his expression terrifies me, and then I am ashamed for pushing him so coolly into this blind and frighteningly raw emotional state. I feel I have made a mistake and regret it. However, strangely enough this incident reassures me about Larry. I see how an appearance of inertia and stupidity can seal off an emotional volcano. I suddenly am convinced he really can learn. To overcome his reluctance, I will have to face leaping fires that lie in wait for his controls to weaken. In another way I fear my blow might have ruined whatever relationship is forming. Probably I feel guilty for taking advantage of my superior strength to force what I believe on principle to be unforceable. At this time I do not have the opinion of Larry's doctor that this moment of physical violence is the turning point. The "spanking" reassures the boy in some very deep spot where lies the fear that an angry adult frustrated by him would literally annihilate him. The blow is actually no more than a light slap on his arm, and the world goes on! Now, I am unaware that this might be the true meaning for Larry. He does not learn any more easily as we go on, and tensions continue to mount. This situation might go on for a longer time but for the fact that Marilyn is sick and has to be out of school for a couple of weeks. It is impossible for me to tutor Larry alone as I must teach classes ordinarily hers. I put Larry and his book at my side while I conduct reading and math classes. He has to learn to read by himself, for I can give him little help and certainly no active instruction. I feel no regrets about this change. No doubt it is also a relief for Larry, who feels too vulnerable when he bears the brunt of my exclusive interest. Concentrating on the group I can hear him mumbling and grunting at my side while the class reads aloud. Out of the corner of my eye I see him ask questions of Jimmy or Amy in math class, and I notice they help him. I hope he is getting somewhere, but I am far too busy to worry about it. He is quiet and apparently hard at work, freeing me to handle more clamorous problems. One day while I talk to Tom across the table to clarify some process in algebra, Larry grabs my hand. I continue talking to Tom, absently letting Larry seize my index finger. He pushes it across his book page for a minute before I realize what is happening. Slowly, laboriously, inaccurately he is sounding out words, one after the other, using my finger to guide him. He is reading! And I've been teaching algebra to someone else!

This is the breakthrough, and as so often happens, the moment and form of its coming seem accidental. Of course it is only the beginning for Larry, and many hours of agonized instruction lie ahead, but it has a great impact on all of us. The students seeing it happen feel encouraged for themselves. I am much moved myself, but feel an extra punch in his "choice" of the math class for his leap forward in reading. The way to his mind still lies along a path where the only guides are refusals and contradictions.

Alden's difficulties with concentration and motivation are as taxing as Amy's or Matt's. His reading and arithmetic are technically as inaccurate as Tom's or Ned's. He needs so much help that we are bound to be disappointed by his failure to come on opening day. During his preliminary interview he had made an ominously sudden shift from resistance against the idea of RSS to complete acceptance. Had we seen this shift as a clue to a dedicated inconstancy, we would have rejected his application. His therapist thinks a lot of headway has been made during the past year of their work together, but as Alden often skips regular appointments, the doctor is doubtful now that he will keep to our program. Our relationship with his doctor is long-standing and he frankly tells us that he is not as close to Alden as he has been with others whom he had referred to us. He does not predict we can help him. Alden's father is even less positive, telling us curtly that he has no idea whether we will ever see Alden again. His attitude is a reminder that however much Alden's parents seem to want him to attend "a school," they do not disguise reservations about ours. A schoolteacher can divine the powerful, subterranean feelings that many adults have against formal education—feelings often far more dogged, whatever their disguises, than the protective resistance put up by students. Alden's two-year absence from school showed his fear of leaving home, and reflected the deeply entrenched attitudes of his parents. Problems of this order are not in our province, but belong to psychotherapy. This period of Alden's life gave free play to his caprice by excusing him from every responsibility. If he now longs for a chance to learn in school and end his narrow isolation, he naturally balks at restraints which school would place on him. He is facing such formidable hurdles that we propose, as a first step leading to our regular program, that he come for tutoring three afternoons a week, after the others go home.

Alden agrees, but it is plain he cannot stick to a definite schedule unless we allow him to play with his airplane models. His doctor recently helped him develop an active interest in building and flying models powered with gasoline motors. Alden's enthusiasm is genuine, and, indeed, models and car-driving are his only interests. But he is seventeen, and his achievement level in school subjects is below the eighth grade; to us his preoccupation with model aircraft during school time seems unsuitable if not ludicrous. We concede that, in the over-all terms of therapeutic goals, his models are a step forward, but in terms of his school problems, they are too suggestive of infantile regressions inconsistent with our program. However, we accept his models as a part of him-as-he-is, as much a part of him as his sulkiness; but we work to get rid of both. It is new and intriguing for Alden to hear us criticize his activities, while we allow them. It is a concrete illustration of the fundamental truth that the teacher-student relationship can tolerate and even thrive on dissent, a concept which astounds all our students.

Alden's afternoon tutoring gets under way after a skirmish when he threatens to stop if his father nags at him to join the regular group. I see how fine is the line between the father's natural impatience and a provocative reiteration of admonitions. My only hope is to find a school subject that may interest Alden enough to let him soft-pedal family vendettas. Introductory algebra draws his attention, and when he has my permission to bring in models and work on them in the afternoon, attendance becomes steady. We are friends, or seem to be. He longs for open relationships, less emotionally loaded than those within the limited circle of his associations. He knows I expect him to join the morning classes soon, and he is content to view tutoring as an intermediate step. Unfortunately, I cannot bring him to focus on learning for more than a short time, and during these moments I often lose the aspect of a friendly person. When I instruct him or review his work, he interprets every correction as a scolding, and suddenly looks up from the page, angrily reproaching me for being just like dear old dad. I answer by saying that he is confused, as his father and I are two entirely different people making wholly different demands. He is bright enough to understand, but his emotions continue to confuse him about me.

Alden seems eager to be a regular fellow, and hopeful of learning algebra. We can see now that he is exceptionally weak, and his resolutions no matter how energetically endorsed are unsteady. His personality is so loosely pegged together and the different layers disengage themselves with such facility that we are still at sea about his real nature. Can it be that behind his self-dramatizations there is nothing solid? I persist in probing for the organic center of his character. Weak students must agree to rely upon the strength of others for a time, eventually learning to stand by themselves.

The regularity of the tutoring schedule established, I praise Alden for his new sense of responsibility. He replies by skipping twice and failing to call in. When he returns his easy vitality seems deflated. He does some homework in algebra, and I praise him again, showing pleasure in his progress. In our next tutoring session he refuses to look at the algebra book, complaining that it is too difficult. Is this negative reaction to praise part of his inner structure? I tell him it is. Our relationship grows stronger. His lapses must be efforts to destroy progress before it adds up to commitment. I believe that my "reading" him and showing acceptance of his backward steps reassure him. His eyes gleam when I discuss the idea of his destructiveness; I do not now ask whether his pleasure comes from the discovery or from the success of his willfulness. It seems obvious that together we are stumbling upon an important piece of knowledge about his way of reacting; such a conclusion seems justified because there is a simultaneous lessening of the tensions between us. He still refuses to come to regular morning classes, but I've made him as ready as I can. Every day I press him to give it a try. In our first interview he showed great interest in Marilyn, and now his questions about her become more frequent. He is also terribly eager for the companionship of boys of his own age. Still, he makes no promises about coming in the morning; to me this is another sign that we are on a more honest footing than we were during the interview. At last one afternoon he "accidentally" leaves his coat behind. The following morning he is there on the front porch at 8:30 waiting for the chance to pick up his coat. After formally introducing him to all the other students, we invite him to stay, and he accepts. He comes every day now with the privilege of leaving again at any hour. Sometimes he takes off an hour after arrival, but these leave-takings seem to be surrenders to inexorable drives to be willful against his will. To our dismay, his parents have recently given him a new car and when he is not distracted by its mechanical vagaries, his already yielding nature is sorely tried by the new and sinister temptations a fast and flashy automobile brings.

Isn't Alden too disturbed for school, and aren't his problems too difficult and deep for solution in the classroom? Like our other students he sees us as enemies while we teach, and wishes he could be our friend. He too suffers from years of inattention to academic learning. He has severe difficulty in reading simple passages and spelling simple words. He suffers embarrassment when these shortcomings receive the limelight. He is invariably more interested in himself than in any subject taught in school; yet he cannot mobilize his energies to make a concerted attack on any of his disabilities. His early withdrawal from school indicates a disaffection more overwhelmingly complete than the usual failures of students to pass courses.

This sets Alden apart. Youngsters like him have found school intolerable because of family relationships which feed on their dependency and weakness. Some years ago we worked with a twelve-year-old boy who had been thrown into a panic by his mother's compulsive need to keep him by her side. After three years at home, helped by extensive psychotherapy, he was willing to try school again. After a few tense days with us, he himself insisted on daily attendance and resisted his mother's sly invitations to stay home. Students like him operate under tensions whose force can be inferred from a picture of this mother's behavior. Every morning when he set off for school, she threw herself across a desk which she pushed in front of the window, and trained a pair of binoculars on his retreating figure. At school his face always fell when he opened the delicious lunch she packed, for he would find written notes and little reminders tucked into every wrapping, so even at midday, she tied him back to her.

Alden suffers a family pressure far more subtle, but equally beyond the influence of teachers—except, maybe, when he telephones in to say he cannot get to school today.

Everyone in the room stops talking and listens to the drama. We all know who is calling and why, as it is nearly time to start the reading period, and there is no sign of Alden. I pick up the receiver and cross my fingers.

"Good morning, Alden. It's almost nine. What's up?"

"I can't make it, Mr. Heinemann."

"Why not?"

"That bitch of a car of mine won't start."

"What happened?"

"Well, I started out all right, but a couple of miles from the house it stalled and wouldn't start again. I'm over at the garage now waiting for them to fix it."

"I'm sorry about it, sort of. But you have to come in anyway."

"How?"

"Come on the MTA, Alden," I urge. "If you want to make it you can."

"Oh, I can't, Mr. H."

"You'd be late but you'd get here."

"No. I won't. It isn't my fault that my car won't run. I told my father that car was no good."

"OK, Alden. Now you've said it. You won't. Is that supposed to determine everything—the fact that you don't *want* to come in? Now, this is just the moment to make a big effort."

"You're trying to make me come in."

"Yes, I am. You know you can leave if you find it's impossible to stay. It's a big job to get you ready for regular school next year. You can't afford to lose even one day with us."

"How'll I get my car?"

"I hope you never do, Alden. You don't have good enough judgment to be driving a car."

"What are you saying?"

"I'm saying you're too upset usually to be driving a car. In your hands it looks more like a weapon. I wish your parents had asked for my opinion before they gave it to you. And besides that I'm saying that I want you to get in here today."

"You must be cracked. I need my car to meet the fellows after school, and honest—I need it to get into school too."

"Take the MTA. It's easy and safe, and hurry up. Don't be later than you have to be."

"I won't take the MTA, Mr. H. Absolutely N.O."

"You're pretty snobby about that, Alden."

"I'll tell you what. I'll be in if I can get my mother's Thunderbird. OK?"

"Not OK. Just get in here right away."

I hang up and wipe my brow as if I had finished a big job.

"Whew! I don't know if he'll come in or not, but he sure makes it hard."

Alden surprises me by showing up after his phone call. He has his mother's car and he bounds into the reading class unruffled and pleased with the world. We postpone discussion because the reading period today has been demanding. Little wonder the students call it Pain Period. They eagerly welcome the half-hour break that follows as a respite. By 10:30 those students who have not eaten breakfast are ravenous; those who smoke are impatient. When a class runs overtime the students can hardly bear it. They fidget and beg permission to smoke or nibble until we formally proclaim the break.

IV ❧ *At Home in School*

DURING EARLY FALL the daily life of RSS might appear to cater to the individual caprices of our students. That their deep needs are inquired into and taken seriously, that the fabric of school days is woven for those needs, reassures them. They had expected condescending airs and cutting retorts. Instead the intense effort to interpret their behavior logically is leading them to a wider self-understanding. They sense a steady underlying purpose. We acknowledge their right to fail, and do not condemn them for exercising it. Not feeling required to achieve academic success, they learn to examine their failures in the light of their experience and goals, so that the discouragement of defeat loses some of its sting. We agree with Tolstoi, who declared a century ago that the student must have the right to refuse those forms of education which do not satisfy his instincts. We want our students to distinguish between the obligation to understand themselves and the pressure to succeed, and now their idea of this difference is growing.

In fact, our day begins before formal classes start. Jimmy, Franny, Tom, and Ned are usually early arrivals, settling down comfortably in the front room with instant coffee to talk about everything. Often serious matters lie beneath the light words; sometimes a student has something important to talk over with us. This morning Franny is standing on the porch, embarrassed but determined.

"Good morning, Franny. I thought you were Ned, and I was just going to give him the blast for bothering me again before 8:30."

"I guess I caught an early train."

"Well, come in. I've got to make a phone call, but make yourself comfortable."

"I'm not too early, am I?"

"As long as it's eight-thirty it's OK."

Franny puts her lunch bag in the kitchen and returns to the front room. She sits stiffly and stares at the floor until I finish telephoning.

"What's the matter, Franny? You look worried this morning."

"Hm . . ."

"Is something wrong?"

"I'd like to ask you something before the others get here. It's about my aunt, the old WrrrrF." Franny grimaces at the thought of her aunt at whose house she often spends the night.

"What about her?"

"She's an old busybody. She gets me so darn mad!"

"What now?"

"It isn't just that. She and my uncle are going to separate for a while. I don't know what it's all about. One thing, though. Dear old Auntie likes to drink too much."

"Is that what's bothering you?"

"Well, sometimes it's pretty disgusting. But that's not what I mean. After all, my uncle has faults, too. He never wants to hear about anything going wrong. They don't talk much, and when their kids are in hot water he won't listen to a word about it. He doesn't even know what his own children are doing."

"Well, Franny, there's nothing new in the situation, is there? You don't know what's really going on between them. Maybe they'll be better off if they separate for a while."

"Maybe they will. No, that's all right. What bothers me is that I don't want to be in the middle. I don't want to take sides, and if I go on staying there I might have to. I'm just not going to be on anyone's side. Let them settle their own troubles. Shouldn't I keep out of their quarrels?"

"Certainly. But it may be hard to. Don't you like your uncle more than your aunt?"

"Yes, but he isn't there so much, and he seems to like it that way. I don't think I'd want to back him up any more than her."

"You want to be neutral, Franny. Maybe you shouldn't stay there now."

"If I don't I'll have to stay at home and see my brother *every* night. Ugh! Besides, the old bat lets me watch TV, and you know my mother doesn't. If I went home every night I couldn't get away with things the way I can at my aunt's."

Ned and Jimmy, followed at a distance by Tom, have come in and they sit down. Tom seems angry at the others, but he looks enviously at Jimmy who is lighting up. His own parents have not given him permission to smoke.

"Franny, do you mind if I tell the boys what we're talking about? It's none of their business, but they'll be wondering and anyway, you'll want to talk about it again."

"OK."

"Franny's aunt and uncle may separate. She's worried that she may have to take sides or give up spending week-nights there."

The boys look at her.and nod. Family troubles are an old and familiar story, and they genuinely sympathize.

"As long as you weren't talking about me," drawls Jimmy. His remark is not just a joke. He suspects that every private conversation is about him, a reflex common in our group. "Where's the bearded wonder?"

"Matt?"

"Who else?"

"He's probably got to go to court again," laughs Tom, forgetting his anger. "I never saw anyone get so many parking tickets. He must go out looking for fireplugs to park in front of."

"He does."

"Oh come on! Why get caught? He has to pay fines!"

"It's not so unreasonable as you think. Who pays the fines for him?"

"His father, I suppose. I doubt Matt earns very much," Tom says sarcastically.

"It sounds funny, Tom, but that's how he gets a reaction from his father. He isn't as lucky as you. He doesn't live at home."

"Lucky! Boy what I wouldn't give for an apartment of my own. Girls, heh! heh!"

"You wouldn't like it if your parents didn't look after things for you."

"N–no. I like to have them to do *some* things for me, but otherwise I want to live my own life."

"I think Matt's stupid about his car," says Jimmy.

"What do you mean?"

"I mean if you use it to drag with or go fast the way you're supposed to, or if you put on the extra equipment yourself that makes it look good and everyone looks at it——"

"Jimmy's right. Man, I saw a street rod last night that was really hot. I couldn't tell whose car it was, but someone sure had blown it. It was a going machine, man—a full race mill," Ned offers.

He like Tom is now anxious for Jimmy's approval. They want to show they are on his side in their familiarity with his world.

"You get pretty excited over all that 'hot' tin. By the way, what does 'blown' mean?" I say.

"Souped up!"

"My old man said he might buy an Impala convertible. What a set of wheels. I can just see me and Baa Baa riding around town in it. Man! Everyone would look at us!"

"Which do you like better, Jimmy, Baa Baa or the Impala?"

"They do different things to me," he leers.

"What are you doing now, Mr. H? Trying to read sex or something into cars? I might have known."

"Why do you all love cars so much? What are they but convenient transportation? You put so much meaning into them."

"That's your twisted mind at work."

"Oh, Mr. Heinemann is talking about Alden. When he gets sore about anything he jumps into his car and drives off like a wildman. What a temper!"

"Mr. H can't get much meaning out of that wobbly English heap of his. It's lucky if it can pass a tricycle!"

"Just like Mrs. B. Those two have to be different from everyone else, in cars, too."

"I want a car to escape the MTA," says Tom.

"Yeah! The subway's the world's worst way to get anywhere."

"Why? What's so awful about it?"

"I hate the MTA. Are the people who work for them feeble-minded or something? Why are the cashiers so slow? They make you miss the trains."

"Yah, and the guards creep up on you just hoping they'll find you doing something wrong."

"I know what Tom hates about the MTA."

"What?"

"The old ladies."

Everyone laughs.

"That figures. You would have to blame women for something. What have you got against old ladies? How could such sweet, little old things make you so angry?"

"Sweet, little old ladies, hah! They get on with their umbrellas and bundles and poke and shove anyone in their way. The other day one of them came right up to where I was sitting and kept muttering that I should give her my seat. When I wouldn't, she poked me with her cane."

"I'm surprised it wasn't a crutch."

"Oh, she was strong enough."

"Yeah! When they don't shove us they give us dirty looks. They expect us to do something bad, and start imagining we've already done it. They don't like us teen-agers."

"You kids have a real complex about old ladies."

"Yeah, I just get mad when I see them."

"Jeez, Tom, you ask for trouble. He was just an asshole today. He was pushing me and Ned around like a nut. And when I had to blow my nose, would he hold my books for me? Oh no! Not him! On the way to Park Street he had his nose up in the air all the way and then he had the gall to call us 'snots' because *we* didn't get off on the same side as *he* did."

"You are a bunch of snotty bastards."

"You walked away from us first, Tom. You were way over on the other platform. And then you wouldn't talk to us."

"OK, boys. What really happened?"

"Well, of course, we did something to Tom first," says Jimmy. "I'll admit that we asked for it when we hid the model engine he showed us. But I offered to fix it for him."

"Yeah, yeah! If you took it home to fix, I'd never get it back. Just like the lawn mower you took. The pieces are still all over your cellar. Ask him! Ask him when he's going to fix it!"

Tom is so eager for friendship and Jimmy knows his own power and uses it. Last week Tom told us that after Jimmy had invited him to spend the night, he took the bed for himself and made

Tom sleep on the floor. Jimmy blushed when Tom told the story, but said he saw nothing very wrong with it.

The air is electric with concern over the yearnings and weaknesses the boys are revealing. At this moment Marilyn bursts into the room with customary verve and energy, her smiles and sparkling eyes undimmed by conflict or tension.

"Good morning, everyone!" she says. "You all look as if the world just fell in."

"Oh, Marilyn. Take it easy. This is progress! Tom's finally standing up to Jimmy."

"I don't believe it. How come?" asks Marilyn.

"Hey, there's Mrs. B!"

"What's in that box you're carrying?"

"My weekly contribution. What you like, I hope."

"Doughnuts?"

"No. Something I made myself. Wait until break time."

Matt and Amy stroll in together, talking, offering greetings to no one, and only grudgingly acknowledging ours. I am about to comment on their manners when the telephone rings.

"Oh-oh," says Jimmy. "I'll bet it's my father."

"Why? What would he call up for?" I ask, reaching to pick up the receiver.

"Checking up. He still thinks I don't come to school half the time, I guess."

"It's probably my mother," says Franny darkly. "She always used to call up my teachers about me."

"I got my parents trained," says Ned. "They aren't supposed to call up without permission."

Eager to learn who it really is, they become quiet. Alden is calling—with another excuse for not coming in. The group listens carefully while I do my best to make him change his mind.

"It's the usual. Now I suppose he won't come in," I say bitterly after hanging up.

"Oh, he'll come in, Mr. H. You talk us into it every time. My mother wants to know your secret," says Tom.

"You know the secret better than I do," is all I answer, puzzled now as always by this reputation for persuasiveness. I should think that it would be easy for them to say "no" when they are safely at home or in a pay station or wherever they are calling from, but evidently this is not so. Perhaps they have an exaggerated sense of the teacher's power, but I believe it is due more to our recognition of their right to refuse—making refusals less necessary—and their growing feeling that we want them to be with us in school. Previously the students were subject to headaches, colds, and stomach disorders that regularly kept them out. Soon after they start coming to our school most of these symptoms disappear. Tom, whose allergies used to keep him home for weeks at a time, hasn't missed a day, and he shows up now even when feverish with grippe. Franny's "nervous stomach" has made only token grumbles. Of course there are times when they are upset about family or personal problems and they do not feel up to a day of study or combat at school. We recognize such feelings and only require them to call up and say what they feel. Ned may still invent a cold when he calls, but the important thing is, he does call. We ask for his real reasons for staying home, but when he won't tell, we ask him to come in and try to work for a while. He always has the assurance that he can leave when he wants to. Telephoning is a big step forward for most students. In September, none of them would have dreamed of it, but then we telephoned them at home when they did not show up. Before long they saw how much they stood to gain by initiating the calls themselves.

When a parent telephones, we try to talk to the student, urging him to come in if he can manage in any way to do so. Parents who have their own reasons for keeping a child at home give vague and ambiguous excuses, confusing to the student. We prefer that the student take responsibility for making his own excuses. Of course decisions concerning absences often reflect the values a particular family sees in education.

Last Friday, Jimmy's mother called to ask us to excuse him on the following Monday. He planned to be at the family summer place on the weekend, and if he had one more day he could finish closing the house for the winter. Otherwise, his father would have to make a special trip to do it in the middle of the week. I replied that we had no wish to interfere with their family arrangements, but we thought school should come first for Jimmy, and we would urge him not to be absent on Monday, leaving the decision up to him. About an hour later Jimmy's father called to protest. He was indignant at our apparent indifference to a practical plan, and wanted us to agree that Jimmy would not miss very much if he was out only one day. He could make it up easily, could he not? I replied that it might be true that he would not miss much academic learning, but if he wanted to solve his school problems he had to stick to our schedule and be here every possible minute. The father became still angrier because he thought we were forbidding Jimmy's absence. We did not forbid it, but I did make it clear that Jimmy ought to be in school even when it might be inconvenient for his family. At last his father conceded that we were not trying to tell him what to do, and, disgruntled though he was, agreed we had the right to express our point of view to Jimmy. Of course Jimmy took Monday off to perform this family chore, but the incident helped lay the groundwork for that wintry day much later when Jimmy would proudly trudge to school two miles through snow so heavy that public transportation stopped and public schools closed down.

Attendance is a crucial issue, establishing the principle that students come to our school voluntarily. The responsibility for organized learning must begin here, if it is to begin at all.

The question of punctuality is far less easily settled than attendance. Without stern reminders, Amy reverts to tardy arrivals. Franny is late when her commuter train is held up, and it is almost impossible to pin responsibility for lateness on her. Alden, Matt, and Jimmy drive cars and complicate their lives with mechanical failures and traffic violations, inevitably reasons for coming late or leaving early. Even when they recognize and freely admit the urgency of their school problems they give priority to the difficulties their automobiles get them into.

The growing influence of cars on the lives of adolescents is attested to as much by the parking lots expanding around high schools as it is by the television shows devoted to car gangsters and explosive squad cars that chase them. It is understandable that when our students feel insecure at home and in school they want all the more to be able to drive a car, onto which they shift personal responsibility. They are dismayed to find that they have to take care of the machine that was supposed to take care of

them. Naturally they say it is not their fault if they are late or
absent after trouble has developed with their cars. The careful
discussion and interpretation of tardiness shows that spreading the
blame is fruitless and ultimately destructive.

For some students who would not or could not go to school at
all, punctuality and attendance have especially crucial meanings.
With Alden, who is in this category, we may handle matters more
flexibly.

"That boy is really spoiled," remarks Matt. "His parents must be
pretty rich."

"Look who's talking," sneers Jimmy.

"Oh, they're really loaded, Jimmy," Tom says earnestly. "I was
out there and the house stretches for miles. He's got a whole wing
to himself, and he has everything—absolutely everything. Radios,
Hi-Fi, motors, old cars—all the stuff he wants."

"They may be rich," says Amy, "but they don't sound as if
they've had it very long. They make too much noise about it."

"They sound just like some people my parents are always trying to get me to spend time with, the Forsythes," Matt sighs.

"Oooooh," squeals Amy. "Do you know Dee Dee Forsythe?
What a riot! Isn't she awful? Always trying to put it on. She
wanted me to go to her coming out party. No thanks!"

"Do you know she actually complained about my sister's boy-
friend sitting on her Ming coffee table in his dirty blue jeans?
Once she made me drive ten miles for a pack of Benson and
Hedges," laughs Matt. He and Amy have put their heads together
over their friends and become happily lost in social geography.

Ned is interested in Alden, and wants to know more about him.
"Why do you let him off the hook when he calls up and gives
a bum excuse like that? You give the rest of us a much harder
time. Especially me."

"You ought to know the answer to that. We don't treat you
all alike. You have different problems, and you're different people," says Marilyn.

"That's right," says Jimmy. "You come down on me pretty
hard if I fake it like that."

"Well, you're strong enough to take it."

"You mean Alden isn't?"

"Yes, but it's after nine, and time for the *Lord of the Flies*. Come on, everyone."

"Wait a minute! This is interesting."

"I know it is, but so is the *Lord of the Flies*, and it's time for it. You can talk about Alden later. Matt, Amy! Break it up. Let's go! Everyone! ! !"

Our kitchen is long and narrow, with an old-fashioned gas stove, an antique refrigerator, and two small tables. When we are all there it is crowded but cozy, with some sitting on tabletops, others standing about, and those with the quickest pickup occupying the chairs. Jimmy, Ned, and Alden rush to the table with their packed lunches and quickly take over the best seats, opening and wolfing their sandwiches in one motion. We teachers follow, turn on water for coffee, and look expectantly for someone to offer us places. No one does, but all eyes are on Marilyn and her cake box.

Once a week she makes an offering to the students, who greedily wait for their share. She stands at the stove to divide a heavily frosted cake and passes it around. After the boys have devoured their pieces, they grin at each other and offer their seats to us.

"At last," laughs Marilyn. "But you had to get your cake first. That's your piece, Bob. Bring it along."

"It looks awfully good, but I don't want it. I'm dieting again."

"You teachers are always dieting. Why don't you lose weight? My parents are always dieting, too."

"I'm the one who never loses. Look how slim Mrs. B is."

"Mrs. B, OK if I go to the corner store?"

"Oh, Matt! Not again! Will you ever bring your lunch? I want you to be here during break. With a minimum of planning you could bring sandwiches."

"If you let us cook here we could bring canned stuff and make things we like."

"You know why I won't let you cook. It's messy and there'd always be a struggle about cleanup. In the end Mr. Heinemann would be doing it. But materials for sandwiches are different. You could keep things like bread and cheese in the refrigerator. Is that all right with you, Bob?"

"Sure. As long as I don't have to clean up after them."

If the students do go out for food, it may take the whole break time before they get back or it may turn a restful period into a confused one. Our paramount consideration is to be with them during breathing spells. The failing student's perceptions in school are likely to be disjointed. In his eyes the teacher in the classroom and the person who is the teacher are discontinuous. Students report that even *they* become different when their hands turn the school doorknob. They change back to "themselves" when they leave again. They like us as persons and they want us for friends, but the moment we begin to teach, our individuality disintegrates for them. The transformation is so compelling they cannot see us as we are even when they want to. We maintain contact during the interval of rest and feeding to establish a unified and continuous view of us whether teaching or not.

"Well, I didn't bring anything this time," says Matt who looks after himself, "and that piece of cake, ugh! They certainly don't know how to bake in the Bronx!"

"I know I can't compete with the culinary products for sale up at the corner, so go ahead, Matt."

"I think you're wrong to let him go like that, Marilyn," I say.

"He loves to go, and I can't stand to see him starve himself."

"That's true, but I think he should be here during the break."

"If Matt can go, Mr. Heinemann, why can't the others?" asks Franny who sits high on a stool apart from the rest. "Mrs. B seems to think it's OK."

Amy's eyes gleam with anticipation. Whether Marilyn and I agree or disagree is carefully watched by all, for they expect us to show either that we are like parents to be played off against each other or that we are like their idea of schoolteachers, mono-lithically arrayed against students whatever the issue.

"Mr. Heinemann has his views and I have mine, Franny," replies Marilyn. "We both agree that each of you has different problems, and it certainly doesn't follow that what we think is good for Matt would be good for you."

"But still, you disagree about some things, don't you?" asks Amy. "How do you settle a real argument? Who's boss?"

"We're partners and neither of us is supposed to be boss."

"I've heard that line before!"

"Why is it a line? We don't always settle our disagreements, but we do try to bring them out so we know where we stand. The more frankly we talk the more likely we are to hit on new ideas. Our personalities are different and there will always be disagreements."

"I know one thing you always argue about. That's about being Jewish," says Amy.

"Right. Mrs. B says I'm Jewish because my parents are, and I say, you can only be Jewish if you believe in the religion or follow Jewish customs. Otherwise you belong to whatever national background you happen to have," I say.

"The Storm Troopers don't ask you what you believe when they drag you away. Besides, there's a lot of important tradition," Marilyn answers. "It goes with being Jewish; you don't have to have religious belief to belong to that tradition."

"I can't deny that. But not everyone has such strong traditions behind him. Anyway my point is that a free man should be able to choose what he is and what he believes. Whatever categories society tries to push me into, I want to choose my own place—if I can."

"Don't you teachers ever stop?" breaks in Ned.

"How come you can always tell somebody's a Jew?" asks Jimmy.

"You can't, you nut," says Franny.

"You can too," chimes in Amy.

"I don't agree," says Marilyn.

"Jews don't look American," says Jimmy.

"What a lousy thing to say," says Amy. "They look as American as you!"

"I agree with Jimmy," says Alden, "there's something about them . . ."

"Do you think you could tell I am Jewish?" asks Marilyn.

"Nnnno . . . Not you. But you're queer anyway."

"What about Mr. Heinemann?"

"With that nose? And that bald head? But I admit he doesn't act it."

"Did I tell you, Mrs. B, that my brother is coming home from college next week?" asks Ned who is unwrapping a neat sandwich and nibbling from a nest of carrot strips and celery stalks.

"Thank God Ned broke up that boring discussion," whispers Alden.

"Is your brother on vacation this time of year?"

"No, he isn't. He is taking some sort of leave."

"That's serious."

"No, it isn't. Lots of kids do it. Besides, my brother's always been the 'good' son. He's the success, I'm the flop. It'll work out."

"In time?"

"That's what they say, but I bet you'd argue about it."

"Why?"

"I don't know. You'd try to make something out of his not going to class lately and sitting around his room playing the guitar."

"Does he play well?"

"Yeah. He's going to play in a folk festival next month."

"My brother's a funny nut," breaks in Alden, between gulps of a tuna-fish sandwich. "Shit! Why can't my mother make a different kind of sandwich? Anyway how could my brother stay in school when I was out? Of course he's immature about a lot of things."

"Stop pulling the light string, Ned. Tom was fooling with it last week, when you weren't here, and he pulled the switch off and on until finally he busted it."

"Did you tell his folks?"

"Of course not. Why should I?"

"Well he was bad, wasn't he?"

"No. Just destructive. I made him pay for having it fixed."

"I thought he didn't have any money. He always says he's broke."

"Well, he asked his father for a bigger allowance."

"Oh, I bet! He wouldn't dare ask his father for anything like that. He's scared to death of his old man."

"I know he is, and at first he said he couldn't ask because his father would hit the ceiling, or him, or something."

"How come he asked then?"

"Oh, Mrs. B and Mr. H told him what to do."

"Like how?"

"Like going right up to the old guy and saying, 'Look, Dad, I really need to have a little more allowance. Can we talk about it?' Something like that."

"What happened?"

"He said he tried it. Instead of blowing up all over the place his old man said he'd discuss it, and before he knew it he gave him more money."

"Ned, now what's making you so nervous?"

"He's probably worrying about getting the business from his brother when he comes back."

"Oh, I'm used to his teasing—sort of. We used to fight a lot when I was smaller. But now we get along pretty well. None of that rough stuff any more. I think he understands me, but I guess he doesn't know so much about himself."

"What doesn't he know?"

"Forget it."

"My kid brother's a mess," says Jimmy, pushing away the remains of his lunch. "I don't know how he does it, but he gets away with things I used to get hell for." He pulls his pile of food back again. He always brings the most generous and fresh-looking sandwiches but he is a picky eater, and after sniffing around, he usually leaves them. He knows we want to share his food but he does not offer it. Sometimes if he runs across one thing he dislikes he just throws the whole lunch away.

"Can I have that sandwich, Jimmy? If you don't want it, I mean," pleads Amy, who has been eyeing Jimmy's operations closely.

"You've already had Mrs. B's cake—and plenty of it," Jimmy observes.

"Oh, come on, Jimmy. Don't be mean. You don't want it. Give it to her."

Jimmy abandons it disdainfully. Amy seizes and devours it. Poor Amy. Her hungry look seems to reflect some feeling that she has been pushed away from her own table while still hollow! We offer her our own food, when we have it, and urge others to do the same. Yet the physical sharing of food does not help her overcome this psychological craving, this infantile selfishness. It does not seem to be a school problem, and we would not take it so seriously if it were not symbolic of Amy's other problems in school. By making it a moral issue about responsibility, we think we can help her understand better what teachers—as distinct from parents—have to offer. We try to convince her that if she takes from us and others, at some point she should give something back, or, if she is unwilling to share, then she ought not to take.

"Amy, please try to bring your own lunch. I know you're hungry," says Marilyn.

"I'm never hungry when I start out in the morning. I don't know. Food isn't that important to me. But what's wrong with eating what Jimmy doesn't want? I keep it from going to waste."

"Well, I think it really is wrong, Amy. It puts you in an awkward position toward Jimmy, for instance. If you keep taking from him, you are going to feel guilty about not giving him something back. It will give him some hold over you."

"Oh, I don't think so. It's nothing to him."

"But it is. Look at him now. He's pleased because he thinks he's already got something on you."

"Maybe you don't want to be responsible to anyone, Amy," I say. "Maybe you don't want to be responsible for yourself either."

"You're making too much out of it. I don't really need the food. I'm not that hungry. You make it sound as if it had something to do with schoolwork."

"Well, sometimes you are perfectly willing to 'take' instruction, but when you're studying on your own, you just quit. So I think it does."

"You know, that just might be so. Sometimes I think—if you want to know—that I would be a lot happier if I didn't have to do a thing."

"Oh, Amy," Marilyn says, "I hope you really don't feel that way. I have an idea. Will you help with the next cake I bring in? You could buy the materials."

"Ugh," replies Amy. "I don't like cake. But maybe. Sometimes when I'm home I make my brothers a cake."

Franny, quietly munching the tomato slices her mother gives her for a strictly low-calorie lunch, has been brooding about brothers, a favorite topic.

"My brother's home, too, heh, heh!"

"Is he sick?"

"Yes, and he's going to be sick for a long time, I hope. They think he has mononucleosis, and am I glad!"

"Oh, not really, are you?" interjects Amy. "Gosh, I'm just crazy about my little brothers."

"Well, nobody tells you how much better they are at everything than you are, do they? That's all I hear at home. 'Eddie talks up in class, why can't you? Eddie gets A's, why can't you? Eddie makes a lot of friends, why don't you?' That's what I hear all the time about my dear brother Eddie."

Matt comes in from the store with a couple of Cokes and two enormous pastry boxes. Sitting down at the table he is surrounded while he opens the boxes. There are a half dozen exotic, fluffy tarts which he devours with complete indifference to his audience, following mouthfuls of goo with long draughts from the Coke bottle.

"Ooooh! Can I have some?" cries Amy.

"After I'm through, garbage pail," snarls Matt. Going out to get food never implies sharing or giving.

Alden jumps up from the table and beckons to Jimmy. "Come on out. I want to show you my new hub caps."

They leave for the street. Amy and Franny wander into the classroom talking about dates. We are alone, enjoying the comparative quiet, drinking coffee.

"I guess the chicken soup therapy is over for this Friday."

Marilyn says, "I suppose it's time to end the break. But I feel like sitting a while longer. If you raise your 'Shall We?' sign, I'll scream."

I have a habit of ending the break with the phrase, "Shall we?" About a week ago Franny brought in a little framed cartoon showing a balding, long-nosed, mustachioed meanie, endearingly labeled, "Our Boss." Underneath she had put in large, bold print my favorite phrase. Now when I want to end the break I just parade around with my sign.

"Wait a minute. Who's in charge of cleanup?"

Franny, hearing the question, returns to the kitchen and immediately starts washing up.

"Franny, it's Amy's turn."

"Oh, I don't mind doing it. I always do it at home."

"Are you punishing yourself here, too? Or just trying to be late for the math class? Let Amy do it."

"No, I'll do it."

The students now talk to us more freely. In the classroom itself, the wars rage sometimes even more violently than at first, but they have made personal contact with us, and are willing to talk about issues and questions that preoccupy them. They no longer fear to reveal feelings about cars, money, movies, superficial relationships with parents and others. They use us as temporary, safe substitutes for parents—often hoping to play us off against each other or testing us to see if we will care for them after they behave badly to us. The students are not yet ready to come to grips with deeper troubles. Willing to hash over episodes with autos, they are not prepared to talk about their real reasons for disliking school. Excessive pressure frightens them. We wait and hope for insights to develop.

The general relaxation during break allows exchanges which throw enough light on character so that we as teachers need not know the content of their deepest preoccupations. Jimmy makes us feel hopeful because he adapts quickly to the kind of analysis we are plugging for. He is furtive and deceitful, but his impulsive and hostile acts are so far not wild or harmful to others. He becomes depressed and less active when upset, but when he learns something about himself or when we are quick enough to sniff out his plots, he is genuinely happy.

By contrast, Franny makes us despair. Her intentions and her morals are better than Jimmy's but she freezes when we expect her to give more friendliness, information, and acceptance of our ideas about independence.

Matt has been upset in the last few weeks. Having moved from a rented room in a respectable house in a "good" part of town, he now lives in an apartment in a run-down section called Amishville. His roommate, Renny, quit Harvard as a sophomore, and has an occasional dishwashing job in the coffee house where Matt hangs out. Amishville is the Cambridge Bohemia for those who can afford expensive apartments, old, in bad repair, but comfortably close to Harvard Square and "The Stick," known as a beatnik cafeteria. Matt's place is a center for wild behavior usually set off by Renny and his middle-aged mistress. Matt stays up late, drinks too much, and eats irregularly. His after-school hours are filled with violent disputes, faithless friendships, and sordid romances. Marilyn and I want Matt to move out and establish a routine to provide for his physical needs. He stubbornly resists change, and however hurt and bewildered he is by his own excesses, he flounders in chaotic group living. Its fascination for Matt worries us. At school both he and Amy take up and run with the ball of psychological interpretation, even though Marilyn tries to confine the issues to school failure. Their shallow sophistication and reckless will to experiment with limits of all sorts make it difficult to assess the real extent of their emotional instability.

We assume that all our students suffer from anxious preoccupations which prevent them from studying, and we have to determine somehow whether they will let us bypass their egotism and lead them to intellectual development. Therapists seldom estimate the degree of success to be expected. We think we can do it with Alden, Matt, and Amy, but Tom may be completely out of reach.

Tom's home hours are spent watching television. He glues himself to movies about monsters and occult terrors, especially late at night. His interest in the bosomy photographs found in various cheap magazines is furtive and fevered. We take it as a serious symptom that he fuses the scatological with fantasies about supernatural violence. In his composition entitled "Noah's Arc," Tom joked about it.

"One day a man invented an instant shit machine. His friend one day accidentally pushed the mass producing button. And soon there were huge tidal waves of shit which soon covered the whole world and every body except Noah's arc and the things in the arc."

In another composition called, "What I Think," he wrote: "What I think about is my friends and their damn dirty minds. Such as Pete Marvin and me. I hate my teachers because they get me all mixed up. My reading teacher makes me read with a machine which I chete on. Then she balls me out. Then I leeve."

He is not in psychotherapy and there is no outside expert to advise us. Superficially he did seem to conform to that class of students with whom our approach had been successful. When we first opened our school we had to face knife-swingers and door-breakers. However, students who lose control with outbursts of frightening violence put themselves outside our province. We are much more influential with sad and withdrawn students who may passively twitch and suffer, but who express strong feelings safely, in words. What if Tom's confused and distorted life-view is of the kind that only psychiatric treatment can right? What if Alden or Ned or Amy can never bring themselves to trust another person? Four of our eight may never learn to give a response from their inner selves or let us befriend them, or eventually learn to study.

V ❦ *The Math Class*

MATH FOLLOWS THE FIRST BREAK. It ought to be a welcome relief from the psychological discussions of the reading period. I say ought to be, because the math we teach is so well-defined a subject that it would seem easy for students to attend to it. Its problems are narrow, and the answers demonstrably right or wrong. "Boring" discussions are unlikely, for it is a no-nonsense subject unconcerned with a dead past or complicated sensibilities. Even girls think of it as neutral territory! Of course we teachers like it because we can use simple, step-by-step procedures which offer almost no encouragement for the distortion of material or the intrusion of vague and irrelevant issues.

Most of the group are studying algebra. Ned, Tom, and Alden are at the beginning. Franny and Jimmy are reviewing their first-year work, and Amy is starting a second-year course. Matt, having completed his high school math requirements before coming to RSS, is studying elementary Spanish in the kitchen.

More than a month has passed since Larry made his great leap into reading, and we have returned him to individual work with Mrs. Hunt during the reading period. It is going slowly, but he is becoming enthusiastic. Unfortunately there is no carry-over into Arithmetic. He blocks now as much over numbers as he did over letters, and Mrs. Hunt agrees that he ought to stay in the math group where we can work for a similar breakthrough. It is slow too, but I think it is coming. Mrs. Hunt, of course, is free to help us teach this complicated set of levels. Each student works at his own pace, and may either stay in one of the rooms with a teacher or get permission to go into a room alone. This offers us an opportunity to give close individual aid in confronting specific academic weaknesses during an organized period. Every effort is made to focus on subject matter, but getting ready is an indispensable, temporizing ritual.

"Tom," asks Marilyn, "have you done the work you took home?"

"Yes, it's done, and I think I brought it in. I just have to find it. I put it on the table somewhere, and it's gone."

"How about you, Jimmy?"

"No. I didn't take anything home."

"Well, do you want to start where we stopped yesterday?"

"Yeah. But I don't seem to get those age problems. Where's my book?"

"I did twenty problems last night, Mrs. B," Ned breaks in. "Here they are. Will you check them now?"

"I can't do it for a little while, Ned, because I have to get the others started. But go ahead and take the answer book. Check the answers yourself, and if you have any questions, ask."

"That wouldn't be right."

"Why not?"

"What if I cheated? I could copy the answers out of the book and you'd never know whether I did the work or not."

"Don't let him have the answer book, Mrs. B," volunteers Jimmy, who cannot miss an opportunity to get something going.

"Well, of course I hope he won't copy out the answers. But if he did, I can't see how that would help him learn how to do the problems, can you?"

"No, I guess not."

"Well then, there is no question of cheating. Go ahead, Ned. Use the answer book and correct your own work."

"Now, Mrs. B," pleads Ned, "you know that's wrong. I never heard of a teacher letting the student use the answer key."

"That's right, Mrs. B," again from Jimmy. "Last year one of my buddies stole the answer book from the teacher's desk, but it didn't do any good. The teacher needed the answers, too, so she used a different textbook."

"OK, Jimmy, you've been heard from. Now will you please do your own work, and let Ned get down to his?"

"Hmmmmm."

"What's wrong? Are you stuck? Ask Mr. Heinemann for help."

"Oh no. I'm all right."

"Well, Ned. Get going, will you?"

"Aw c'mon, Mrs. B. It's your job to correct my work. That's what you get paid for, isn't it? And we pay plenty, too."

"No, Ned, that's not what I get paid for. I get paid for helping you solve your learning problems. And if your arithmetic is good enough to let you multiply the tuition by 8, you can see for yourself that we don't earn very much at that."

"Well, let's see now, 1600 times eight. . . ."

"You'll have to divide the result by two after subtracting expenses."

"$12,000 between the two of you."

"Don't forget Mrs. Hunt has to be paid."

"Well, it's not so much I guess. But how do you get the money for your cars and your trips and everything?"

"My husband is the real earner in our family. So, you see we're not making a fortune out of you. But enough of that. To work with you."

"Well, whatever you make, you're a teacher, and teachers are supposed to correct our work. I won't do it myself. It's wrong."

"I can't do it now, Ned, and if you're going to insist on my doing the checking, you will have to wait until I have the time."

"I'll wait."

"You'll have to work while you wait, Ned. Here, I'll give you some more equations with fractions to clear. These examples will be just like those you did at home."

"OK."

"Now! After all that talk, I don't see the answer book. Does anyone know where it is?"

"It was right here in the middle of the table yesterday."

"It's gone now."

"Mrs. B, is it all right if I help Tom with his work?" Franny asks.

"What are you going to be working on, Tom?"

"Oh, I'll try some more of those examples about adding and subtracting signed numbers. I'll go ahead while you check my homework."

"All right, Franny. Help him if you can. But it may be harder than you think. Let me know how it goes. Tom, if you'll hurry up and find your homework, I'll check it for you," Marilyn says. She corrects Tom's work first because he is the least able to work independently. Tom's confusion over algebraic concepts requires the closest possible supervision.

They stir about looking for misplaced textbooks, wandering answer books, and forgotten homework papers, slowly settling down to work. I sit beside Alden to push him today's step into algebra. Yesterday, staying through the whole school day, he filled out about a week of uninterrupted attendance. Then this morning he called in again, presumably from home, and we argued about whether he should come in. He made it, but he is in a nervously excited state. He seems to like algebra, but his interest is too weak to encourage him to work independently. Amy is with me too, but she is efficient about her books and work, finding everything she needs in a moment. She has no qualms about using the answer book and seems happy that we trust her with it. Larry is struggling with a workbook he cannot read. These three can easily take up all my time. Mrs. Hunt is in the kitchen helping Matt get organized.

In September he and Amy insisted on my teaching them French which they had studied before. Both had been to boarding schools where instruction in Latin and French begins early and repetition is the automatic cure for failure. To them a school without French was unthinkable. Unaware of this, and glad to have the chance to teach French, I thought we could read Molière with real pleasure because of Matt's love of acting, but French was too closely associated with other loathsome school demands to which they had been giving outward compliance. Amy dissolved into helplessness right away, and could hardly reproduce a single French sound. Matt's knowledge of French is adequate and his talent for languages above average, but he would only stare at the words and giggle insultingly at Amy's floundering or my urgings. I was just left there with Molière all to myself. When I turned to French grammar, they got even more stubborn. At last Amy abandoned the project and Matt admitted that French took him back to experiences he sought to escape. Any interest he might have had in Molière was drowned in this flood of feeling. Amy turned to math and Matt to Spanish as an entirely new subject. He follows the textbook himself, and we teach him only when he asks us to.

Everyone is busy with his own work. Each has the reassurance of knowing he is engaged in the same general activity as his fellows, whose demands for individual attention protect his privacy; he can summon almost the whole attention of one or even both teachers when he wants it. Pressure is not to finish the course but to grasp and learn a particular principle or process.

Of course this is not the way the students *feel* it. The hand of the past is heavier than lead, and no matter how logically or impersonally or repeatedly the textbook states that B follows A, the memory of old experiences reminds them that authority menaces behind all requirements.

Marilyn is still searching for her answer book. Alden, waiting for me to prod, listens in to more active developments in her room.

At last he calls, "Where would you teachers be without that answer book?"

"We'd be lost. You're wasting a perfectly good sneer, though."

"We never claimed to be experts in algebra. If we can figure out how to do problems by using all the clues, we can teach you. Sometimes that's the best way to teach," I say.

"I still don't see how you can teach a subject if you aren't really good at it yourself."

"Well, we're getting good."

"If you see me figure out how to solve problems, you can learn to use your head the same way. Instead of my telling you what to do—which you always hate—you can find out for yourself."

"Why do you want to make it so complicated? You're supposed to show me what to do and tell me to do it. Then I work it over and you correct it and give me a mark."

"Why do you pretend it isn't complicated? If I tell you what to do you bristle. If I try to show you how to do things you feel that I'm making you small, don't you?"

"Well, yes. Isn't that what you're trying to show? Teachers want to be big and show off that they're better."

"No, Alden. You're wrong," says Marilyn.

"See! See! That's what I mean. If I tell you what I think you say I'm wrong."

"Well, in this case you *are* wrong. I teach you because I want you to learn. I am stronger, and we both know it, and a person who is strong doesn't need to prove it."

"Yeah."

"OK. So you can't stand it if I teach you. Why don't you jump at the chance to learn how to figure things out on your own?"

"Click, click," Alden lifts his hand to his ear and makes a turning motion. "Now you're turned off."

"You and Mr. H are just trying to get out of work with that jazz. The same as when you told me to use the answer book myself," interrupts Ned.

"Hey, Ned, I thought you were working."

"How can I concentrate with all the noise you guys make? Can I go in the front room and work by myself 'til you correct my homework?"

"Work by yourself!" snorts my partner.

"Uh oh! Watch out, Ned," says Jimmy. "The Tank is getting ready to roll. She'll flatten you."

"You didn't call me a tank when I brought in the cake."

"I didn't call you a tank at all, Mrs. B," protests Ned.

"Sometimes I wish you would, Ned. I know you think I am one often enough."

"Well, I wouldn't say that, Mrs. B."

"No. Maybe you will though."

"I just think you use the wrong methods with us."

"All right, Ned. I have a notion that you won't be able to work any better by yourself than you do here with us. You're unusually restless today, and I don't know why. But maybe you're just angry about my methods, as you say—though I doubt it. Show me. If you refuse to correct your homework yourself, get busy with the exercise I gave you. Stay in here until you really understand the equations. Then go along into the front room. I'm sure you can handle fractions without help."

Delaying actions are coming to a close. Marilyn has found an extra answer book, and turns to correct Tom's homework. Five or ten minutes pass with each person engrossed in work. Franny is still helping Tom, and they murmur quietly to each other. Jimmy is almost as distracted by quiet as by conversation, and keeps looking up from his book to see whether everyone is actually studying. At last he catches Ned staring abstractedly into space. He returns to his own work smiling, satisfied that basically things are pretty much as unsettled as he likes them to be. When again Ned takes up pencil and paper, it is to draw a doodle of a horned Viking helmet with laundry hanging from a line stretched between the horns. He draws it in careful detail revealing both talent and skill. This concentration draws Tom's attention and he and Ned giggle together. But Tom turns back to his work, and Ned continues doodling a bit longer. He yawns, and leaning back in his chair, slips down. At last he reaches for all the books lying loose on the table and piles them in front of him, facing Marilyn. When the piles are high enough, he sinks behind them, pillowing his head on folded arms.

"Damn it!" explodes Jimmy. "I can't figure this out. Come here and help me, Mrs. Bernstein."

"All right, Jimmy. But if you're in a big hurry you could come over here instead of making me jump to you."

"OK, but I need help, so just come."

Jimmy has trouble with word problems, and even when he understands the mathematical relations which the words describe, he lacks self-confidence, suspecting and doubting his own insights. Marilyn goes over and sits beside him. She praises and encourages him for his work so far. Then, to master the problem, she shows him how to write each verbal element algebraically.

For example, if the problem says that a father is twice as old as his son, Jimmy must write down that the son's age equals x and the father's $2x$. Slowly making a list of correct algebraic phrases to match verbal ones, he can easily coordinate them. Jimmy hates to write things down. In his haste to be done with a problem he scornfully telescopes the elements, and then loses the scent, forgetting some fact, which throws him off. Marilyn shows him repeatedly that when he does write things down carefully he solves problems with ease.

"But it's so stupid, Mrs. B, to write down $2x$ like that. I know it anyway. I can keep it in my head," complains Jimmy, who shares the view—with most of our students—that intelligence is measured by speed, facility, and efficiency. Our society links hard work with character building on one side, and intelligence with quick returns and easy living on the other. Jimmy is the kind of sporting-life person who puts them together by equating intelligence and shrewdness. As a potential con-man, he is afraid to let the teacher take him in even to solve a problem! However, this time he reluctantly agrees to follow her suggestions. Ned is now sound asleep. Tom and Franny are giggling about it.

Marilyn turns from Jimmy, saying, "What's the matter, Ned? You're not doing anything and I won't let you go to sleep here. Go home, if you're too tired to work."

"Mrs. Bernstein, I'll do the examples, but not here."

"Why not?"

"I want to go to the next room and be by myself. I can concentrate better there."

"Why can't you concentrate here?"

"It's too noisy."

"Is that the only reason?"

"Of course."

"Why were you going to sleep if the noise bothers you so much?"

"I wasn't really asleep."

"I've noticed that you get sleepy when you've got something on your mind. You certainly are more distracted than usual. What is it, Ned?"

"It isn't anything. You're making another wrong guess. All I want is to be alone in the next room. I'll do my work there."

"Oh, c'mon, Ned."

"Oh, c'mon, Mrs. B."

"You're getting angry, aren't you?"

"Just irritated. Not angry. Please, Mrs. B."

"OK, Ned. Let's try it. You seem upset to me, but if you can work in there by yourself, go ahead."

Relieved and pleased, Ned carefully picks up his book and some loose papers, and shuffles off into the next room. He yawns once again, and my partner shakes her head skeptically, turning back to Jimmy. He huddles over his work, arms stretched down under the table and shoulders nearly touching his papers. Although red in the face, his attitude toward algebra is distant, petty, affectedly proper.

"What happened, Jimmy? Do you want me to help you?"

"No. No. It's OK. I just got it. I don't need you," Jimmy replies, sitting up and trying to look pert again. He is tired of full attention. Marilyn turns back to Tom's homework which is distressingly full of errors. Yesterday she worked hard with him and thought he understood about adding and subtracting signed numbers. But Franny's call for help interrupts.

"I can't get Tom to do this right. I've explained it and told him what to do, but he gets it wrong half the time. Can I do my own work now, please?"

"Yes, Franny. I can get you started if you want."

"Do you think it would be all right if I just go ahead with the next factoring exercise?"

"Let's see . . . Don't do all of them, though."

"Why not? That's what I was taught to do—do all the exercises."

"You can if you want to. But I'd do every odd one, say. It would be just tiresome to do them all."

"I don't think I should skip any."

"All right. Tom, come here and we'll correct these together."

Marilyn's students are temporarily serene. Meanwhile I have just finished explaining to Larry his assignment in the workbook. He has to learn "addition facts"—that is, that 3 and 5 produce the same sum no matter which way they are added. Following the instructions of the workbook to the letter, I am trying to make it possible for Larry to work without constant supervision. The stiff formality of the requirements has a special reassurance for him. Amy seems happy with her work, and I am especially glad that this is so because she is doing a complicated kind of factoring difficult for me to follow. If she gets into trouble, it takes all my concentration to follow the process to the point where she is lost. Alden fidgets, unable to decide whether he regrets coming in. We are beginning to worry about what lies behind these doubts, for they do not seem to be diminishing. Earlier we took his morning refusals and early departures from school more lightly on the grounds that his coming to school with any regularity at all was a big step forward. Yet, experience with others who had also had extended vacations from school responsibility told us that "gradualism" as Alden was practicing it might be exaggerated. Generally, if they came at all after two or three weeks they stayed. Alden seems too strongly attached to his ambivalence.

I give Alden his assignment and feel certain that he knows how to handle it—simple substitution exercises and easy equations at the beginning of the text. While I talk to Larry and Amy and look in on Matt and Mrs. Hunt in the kitchen, Alden seems to be working. At last I sit down next to him and give him the help he needs. He is perfectly used to me, but inches away from the possibility of physical contact, fearful of a close human touch. But he is a little proud of starting to learn algebra, and this is a kind of motivation. I look hopefully where he has been writing, only to see that when I took him to be working he was decorating the textbook page entitled *Instructions to the Teacher*. To the left above the title he has drawn a stick figure walking the plank, and an arrow points from the word "teacher" to the figure. Another stick teacher stands on a gallows with a noose around his neck. On the right, below, is a drawing of a hand with extended finger, and under the word "Instructions" he has written "Eat it."

"OK, Alden, I'm in for it. Are all those meant for me?"

"Maybe."

"Well. It's a safe guess you're in a bad mood—to say the least."

"You bet."

"Let's do some work. Maybe you'll get over it."

"I don't know. I'm pretty miserable."

"No one here has had a chance to make you feel that way."

"You made me come in here."

"How could I have made you?"

"Well, you put it pretty strongly on the telephone."

"Do you mean that I threatened you?"

"Not in so many words."

"Not at all, Alden. I only told you that in my opinion you should come in. You did, and I am very proud of you for making the effort. But you don't need to stay. Go, if you don't want to try to work at all."

"Are you serious?"

"Of course."

"I didn't come all the way in here against my will just to leave right away."

"Good."

"OK. Let's do some algebra. As a matter of fact I tried this one, but I didn't know what to do. What does that little 2 mean?"

In explaining, I cannot drop a didactic tone which always sets Alden on edge. He just stops listening. Aware of this I lead him back to practical exercises, determined to "instruct" as little as possible. If he bogs down, I'll just help him out. The problems give set values for x and y, and all he has to do is remember what they are, and combine them through multiplication, addition, and subtraction. If he forgets the values he can look them up. Unfortunately he gets mixed up, and his answers are usually wrong. He gives no grounds for praise and encouragement.

I urge him to write everything down carefully, but that edge undoubtedly comes back into my voice. At last he explodes,

"Oh, Mr. Heinemann, that's too stupid. I can do it in my head."

"You're not doing it right your way. Why not try mine?"

"That would be giving in. Besides it will make me feel stupid to write all that stuff over and over."

"You should try to be very careful to follow each step closely and go slowly until you really know what you're doing."

"How will I ever get through it, then?"

"If you try to go too fast before you . . ."

"Haste makes Waste? You sound just like Dad."

"Does he try to teach you?"

"God, yes. I can't stand it. Hey, do you have to sit so close? What smells?"

"Oh, come on, Alden. Let's get on with it."

"OK. Give me another one."

"Number three. What does $2xy$ equal?"

"Hmmm. x is 4 and y is 5."

"Yes."

"I multiply all of them?"

"Yes. Write each number down."

"Oh, I don't need to. Let's see—I don't know. I can't do that."

"Why not, for heaven's sake?"

"I don't know my tables."

"You mean you don't know what 4 times 5 is?"

"It's not 16, is it?"

"No. Well, you'll have to learn the multiplication tables."

"Oh, come on. That's too childish. You said you'd teach me algebra."

"I know I did. But I thought you knew enough arithmetic to be able to do simple multiplication. It's no disgrace not to. But you'll have to learn the tables before we continue."

"You've gone too far. NO! I WON'T go back to that kid stuff!"

But Alden will have to memorize the multiplication tables well enough to recite them. Old-fashioned, rote drills provide an ordered discipline through which Alden can acquire mastery of a limited field of knowledge. This raises a psychological issue of especial importance to the student of middle class background, who develops an intellectual "style" to express social ambitions. Our culture—or one aspect of it—puts a premium on the facility with which every sense experience is converted into an idea or concept. The idea is needed for exchange in social intercourse. What counts in regard to these "instant" ideas is their social value, which encourages people of limited understanding to echo them with little respect for content. Sometimes the student comes to believe that a concept does him credit just because it *is* vague and flat, for thus he shows a conspicuous disdain for the gathering and evaluation of details. Routines, scheduled inspection of experience, perseverance are for clods, not for people with "brains"! This depreciation of intellectual values dovetails perfectly with the willfulness of students already pretentious and reluctant to give themselves over to discipline. Several of our students engage in, and all are affected by, this imitation of learning.

Learning the multiplication tables by rote seems too humble a way to combat a serious disorder. Why do we not take advantage of the new curriculum changes developed to improve and accelerate instruction in math? Could we not raise intellectual values by teaching a new kind of math designed to induce students to reason for themselves, to understand concepts rather than memorize rules? Such revisions in the curriculum have little if any bearing on the problems of our students, who are too distracted to be stimulated by ideas. Before they begin to cope with new concepts they need to develop self-discipline. At RSS the multiplication tables happen to provide material for clashes between students and teachers over the nature of a specific learning task. Several years ago I worked for an entire summer with an unusually bright and sensitive thirteen-year-old who said that all his academic difficulties would clear up if he could only learn the "tables," a prognosis first made by the independent preparatory school he attended. It was impossible to believe that any learning task would be too difficult for this boy, and yet he did seem wholly baffled by the "tables." At the end of the summer he knew them, but it took most of that time before he could decide that he *wanted* them. Thus, we aim for a clarification of the issue of willfulness before seeking a method to catch the student's fancy. We want students to be inspired and inventive, but these qualities are not vitiated by submitting to the discipline of a subject. So, we insist with Alden.

"Alden, there is no choice. You'll have to learn this 'kid stuff.' "

"The hell with that! I want to learn algebra."

"You can't learn algebra unless you know how to multiply. I won't try to teach it to you until you learn your tables. As soon as you can multiply easily and correctly we'll return to algebra."

"Go away, Chrome-Dome. You make me nervous."

"What are you going to do about it?"

"I don't know. I'll think about it. Don't call me, I'll call you."

Alden needs time. Larry is looking at us hopefully and I go to look at his work. As long as he goes slowly his simple addition is correct, but when he finishes the exercises he needs help with a word problem. We can hear Marilyn talking to Tom in the next room. Franny is restless. Jimmy cannot work without frequently checking on the others. Twice he has gone to the pencil sharpener and once into the kitchen for a drink and a quick look at Matt and Mrs. Hunt, who are talking seriously, but so softly that even Jimmy's hearing is not acute enough to pick up the drift. Jimmy's suspicion that private conversation concerns him has not been much allayed, and his cocked ears sabotage his concentration. Now he observes Ned stretched out on the couch in the front room staring out the window.

"Ned sure is getting a lot of work done," he comments. "Hey, Ned! Are you taking a little window therapy?"

"Shut up, Fink! Can't you mind your own business? I'm doing algebra," Ned turns away from the window to look back at his book.

"Mrs. Bernstein, I thought I could do these problems, but none of them comes out right," Franny calls. "What's wrong with this one?"

"Let's see," says Marilyn, moving over to Franny. "The factoring looks right. You'd better let me look at the book for a minute."

"What if you couldn't do it yourself, Mrs. B?"

"I'd ask Mr. Heinemann. Between the two of us we could probably figure it out."

"But what if you couldn't?"

"Well, maybe you could find out the answer at home. Doesn't your father know algebra?"

"Oh yes."

"This time I don't have to figure it out, Franny. You made your usual mistake."

"What do you mean?"

"You copied the problem incorrectly. That's careless in the true sense—not being able to care less."

"Hmmm. But I care. I do want to learn algebra."

"Why?"

"Well, my mother says . . ."

"OK, Franny. But if you were interested in the subject for yourself you would take pains to guarantee that you copied your problems correctly. It's like your spelling."

"I see my mistake now. I'll try again. Should I do all the others on this page?"

"You know what I think about that."

"Well, I'll do them all, no matter what you say."

Marilyn turns back to Tom. She does not keep the irritation out of her voice.

"Tom, this homework is almost all wrong. It looks as if you didn't understand what we worked on yesterday. I was sure you did."

"I thought it was right."

"Did you know you were running into trouble when you were doing them last night?"

"Well, yes. I felt something was off."

"Why didn't you call me up and ask me about it?"

"I didn't think you'd want me to call you after school."

"Why not?"

"Well . . ."

"Don't try to say you wanted to spare me! The fact is the last thing you would want to do is to call up a teacher after hours."

"Yeah. You've got it, B. When I step out that door, I become me again—and that lets you out, Teach."

"But even when you're 'you,' you want to get your work right, don't you?"

"Yes, I do."

"It's a waste of time to do this kind of work. I think I could have straightened you out over the telephone. It would have been worth a try."

"Me, call a teacher? That would be getting pretty friendly."

"Well, yes. But aren't we friends in school?"

"Skip it! Correct the work."

"Well, don't forget. Whenever you have a problem about your homework, I invite you to call me—before ten of course—and ask me for help."

"Fat chance!"

"Now, let's look at this problem. Do you remember the rule about the subtraction of signed numbers?"

"Yes. That's the one where you used a thermometer for the minus numbers."

"Right. Do you remember that in any subtraction problem one number is the minuend and the other is the subtrahend?"

"Yup. The bottom number is the subtrahend. You said sub was under."

"Good. You must have known what to do to get some of these

examples right. But too many are wrong. Why didn't you use the same reasoning on all the problems?"

"Well, look, Mrs. B, in this one the bottom number is bigger than the top one, isn't it?"

"Yes, it is. But why worry about that? You can have minus quantities."

"But you can't take away a large number from a small one. You always take the small one away. Otherwise it goes against what I learned a long time ago."

"But, Tom, in algebra some ideas are different from what you learned in arithmetic. You yourself tied minus numbers into the thermometer idea."

"Yeah. I get that bit. But the book is wrong about taking away big numbers. You're wrong, too. I know what I learned in arithmetic and you can't change my mind."

"But, Tom, you agreed that minus quantities made sense!"

"Why should I believe you? I know that rule I learned must be true. Besides, my father reminded me of it when he helped me with my homework."

Tom's intelligence is cooped up in a homemade prison and his father has the key. Tom wants to learn algebra, and would like to follow the teacher, but cannot accept a principle which violates an earlier idea sanctioned by his father. He is shocked by the prospect of a conflict between authorities. When he ran into it over his homework last night, he did a few examples according to the new rule, and the rest according to the old. He tried to ignore the contradiction of the two ideas, but when forced to choose he favors his father. Tom's truculence and intransigeance only hint at the emotional tangle behind his confusion. But he has revealed enough to suggest that students who stubbornly cling to what they know, may appear to be slow, even disabled learners. Right now we are at an impasse. Tom angrily refuses to take Marilyn's word for the truth of what she knows and teaches. It is a personal challenge, in a way, and moreover a defiance of reason, and she becomes more insistent. Tom's sullen expression changes to a smirk when he sees her frustration. Alden, listening to the argument, tries to break the mounting tension.

"Mr. Heinemann, how did you get so bald?" he blurts out,

laughing. Ned, having left his couch, listens in the doorway, and his laughter joins Alden's.

"I don't know. It's just inheritance, I guess. Is that your answer to the question of learning the multiplication table?"

"Well, you know me. I was thinking of something else. You have so little hair that you probably give each one his own name," he giggles. Everyone smiles. "Who's on the sick list today?"

"Ned! What are you doing back here?"

"I don't want to miss the jokes. Or the arguments."

"You begged to be allowed to go into the front room because we were making too much noise for you to study in here. What a faker!"

"Well, you still haven't corrected my work, have you, Mrs. Bernstein?"

"No, Ned. I have not. But I want to know why you're not doing your work. You've had your chance to do what you said you wanted. But it seems that you can't do what you want, or you don't really want to do what you say. Which is it?"

"All right! All right! Forget it. I'll go back to work."

"Mr. Heinemann, I can't figure this out at all," Amy calls out. "Come, quick!"

Amy, bent over her work, is chewing her fingernails. She is good at math, proud of this link with her father, a gifted designer and engineer. Although not as quick as she is at intermediate algebra, I can usually find her error when she is in trouble. Testing my wits that way sets a good example for her because despite the motions she shrinks from independent work. Now, she is hung up on a factoring problem, and, going slowly, we each discover how to do it at about the same time.

"Let's check it in the answer book, Amy."

"I'll look it up," she says cheerfully. "Yup! We're right, but I think they used a different method in the book. But it works either way."

"Good. I was hoping we wouldn't have to fight our way through it again. I was afraid we would make a mistake in adding or something like that. When I hurry my addition is rotten."

"Do you want me to go on with the next example? It looks like the same idea."

"Yes. I think you're all set now for the rest of the exercise."

"Mr. Heinemann, can you come into the kitchen for a minute?" asks Mrs. Hunt, whose talk with Matt has been uninterrupted.

"Matt can't get down to work. He's got something on his mind, and I don't know what to say."

"OK, Mrs. Hunt. Everything's going well here. Keep an eye on Larry for me. He seems to be getting pretty sore at his workbook. Alden's still sulking and Amy's working."

"Wait a minute, Bob." She takes me aside; "Matt's talking in a pretty wild way. I better warn you."

"Thanks, Josie. It's not the first time."

In the kitchen, Matt, alone with his Spanish book, is gazing into space.

"What's up, Matt?"

"Did Mrs. Hunt tell you?"

"Only that you've got something on your mind and can't study."

"Do I have to learn these verb endings? It seems foolish."

"Matt! I know you're not studying them because you're thinking about a problem."

"You're smart, Mr. Heinemann. You can read my mind, I suppose?"

"No, I can't. I already said Mrs. Hunt told me."

"Do I have to be here when those other kids are? They bug me." Matt begins to giggle.

"OK, Matt. You're angry. Why not just say so? I'm not going to be suckered in by your false starts. If you keep this up, you might as well leave."

"That's not it, Mr. Heinemann. I mean I'm not angry."

"Then what's behind your not studying?"

"I guess I'm afraid to tell you." His giggles have stopped.

"Tell me what?"

"That's just it. You might get sore."

"Is it important? Is it keeping you from studying?"

"Yes, to both."

"You'd better tell me anyway. You know me well enough to know what makes *me* angry—your fakery."

"Shall I tell you what I'm thinking about?"

"Of course."

"Do you know what peyote is?"

"Vaguely. Some kind of drug, isn't it?"

"It's not really a drug. I mean you don't get addicted to it."

"What does it do?"

"Well, first it makes you feel awful! Then your barriers go down. I mean your subconscious seems to spread out like a flower. You get all sorts of images that ordinarily you repress. It's in color, too. I mean you see the most intense colors along with your dreams. There's a lot of experimenting going on in Harvard Square. Some kids are even sniffing cough medicine, for kicks. Haven't you read about the experiments they did with Harvard students?"

"With LSD? Yes. But I thought that these things would be controlled."

"Oh, they're not bad. They're supposed to help you understand yourself better. Did you ever hear of—what's his name? He writes books, and lectured at MIT. Huxley! That's it."

"Yes. I've read some of his novels."

"Oh, Mr. Heinemann," calls Amy. "I need you. I just can't do this problem. Please come help me."

"All right, Amy. I'll come. Damn it, Matt, that girl knows perfectly well how to do that problem. She just doesn't want to do it by herself. Well, look, I don't know anything about drugs except one thing. You must not experiment with them or take them for any reason. Is that what you wanted to talk about?"

"Yes. I'm really interested in drugs. Besides, if it's true that your subconscious gets freer I might be able to speed up my therapy. Anyway, I want to see what it's like."

"I'm sure Mrs. Bernstein feels just as strongly as I do, Matt, that you should not do it. I'd like to continue this discussion, but I think she ought to be with us and it must be private. I don't want this to become general talk. The other students should not be involved. Can we put it off until later in the day?"

"Certainly."

"You haven't begun these 'ejercicios' have you? Or the 'Como se dice' section? Well, then for now just write out the present tense of the three conjugations. I'll come back shortly to check. I'll talk to Mrs. Bernstein about the peyote question and we can sit down together before she leaves."

"Mr. Heinemann," wails Amy. She is interrupted by a loud thump and scuffle. Her howl changes to a surprised exclamation, "Wow! Larry!" This is followed by the loud slam of a door.

"I'll do the exercises first, Mr. Heinemann. I know those verb endings all right. I feel better. Thanks for talking to me."

"I'll be back," and I hurry to the scene of the noise. Amy is looking excitedly about her; Alden stares out the window; but Larry is gone.

"What happened? Where's Larry?"

"Oh, you should have been here, Mr. Heinemann."

"Yeah, Larry came to life."

"What do you mean? Where is he?"

"He ran outside."

"Why?"

"Well, he was just sitting there staring at his book. His lips were moving but he didn't say anything. All of a sudden he picked up his workbook and threw it against the wall and swore like anything."

"He jumped up and ran out, slamming the door behind him."

❦

Outside Larry walks slowly toward the corner. His head is down, and he looks miserable.

Hurrying to him, I take his arm, saying, "It's all right, Larry. Really it is. No damage is done. Come back with me and let's talk."

"I want to go home."

"You can go home after we talk about it. I don't want you to go home feeling so bad."

"Aren't you sore?"

"Not at all. Just the opposite. I've been hoping you'd let your feelings out a little. I think you've done a great thing."

Larry stops, and turns to look at me, trying to understand. His great brown eyes are full of tears, and though they splash down his face he looks steadily at me.

"Yes, Larry, I know. You've wanted to do that for a long time, haven't you? Now you've done it and you haven't hurt anyone, and it's all right. Come back. If you feel like tearing up the workbook, go ahead. They don't cost much, and it would be worth it to have something to take out your angry feelings on. I've got some used ones you can practice on."

Larry begins to smile at last, and he takes the time now to wipe away his tears.

"It's all right to cry, too, Larry. I would, if I felt like you."

Returning to the room, we sit down. Amy looks at Larry and smiles sympathetically, while Alden comes over and says, "I'm glad you came back. Watch out with those explosions, or you'll be competition for me."

"Now, Larry, what made you so angry?"

He drops his head, overcome again with embarrassment. But he does not answer.

"Were you angry at me, or was it the book?"

"The book."

"Why?"

He looks at me out of the corner of his eye, but is mute.

"Did you hate it?"

He nods, and his eyes glisten again.

"I can't get it."

"Does the book remind you of something that happened to you in school before?"

"Yes."

"What?"

He re-enters his silence, looking grim.

"I'm glad you threw the book. Are you?"

"Yes." The tears are flowing again; the tension is gone.

"Good. Now what's next? You don't need to go home now, do you?"

"No."

"All right. Alden, you help him a bit with the math, if you can. If you can't do it, I'll give you some mechanical drawing exercises to do. Alden can read you the instructions."

"I'll try the math again. But I don't want to use that book."

"Here's another, then. See what you can do adding these examples. Now, Amy, what did *you* want?"

"Me?"

"Didn't you call me out of the kitchen?"

"Yes. I forgot. I need help. I don't know how to factor this."

"Why, Amy! You haven't done even one problem by yourself."

"I know."

"Well, at least you're clearing the air a little."

"What do you mean?"

"Your story about how much better you'd learn if you had individual instruction is as untrue as your story about how much you want to learn."

"But I do want to learn."

"Why don't you learn how to do these problems when I sit down and work them through with you? I learn that way, and I should think you would, too."

"I don't know why I don't. I'm just dumb, maybe."

"Dumb like a fox, Amy. You're a very intelligent girl."

"Shrinks would say maybe it has something to do with having you help me."

"Maybe so, but that means that you're putting that 'something' ahead of your interest in math."

"Say, Bob, is Larry all right? I thought I'd better stay out of it. I knew something was going to happen."

"Oh, Mrs. B," calls out Tom, "is the period almost over?"

"Fifteen more minutes, Tom."

"Mrs. B, will you check these for me?" asks Franny.

"You did these just now? But they're all alike, Franny. It's as if you did the same thing over and over again long after you knew how to do it."

Franny blushes violently and says, "I thought if I did the work—"

"Mrs. Bernstein, you take the cake," breaks in Jimmy. "Any normal teacher would be pleased she did all that work. Instead, you give her the blast."

"Jimmy, you're listening in again."

"Why do you all think you're being good if you are working? Busy-ness doesn't have much to do with learning. Work by itself is meaningless."

"I get it," snorts Alden. "She doesn't want Franny to do all that work because she'll have to correct it."

"My God! What ideas you have about me and what I want! It's true that I don't like to correct a lot of dull homework, but I'd certainly do it if it helped my students."

"Well, it does. It means you're doing your job. We do the work and turn the stuff in. Then you have to correct it and grade it."

"That's not my idea of being a teacher!"

"It's unfair to give Franny the blast after all that work!"

The discussion gets hotter, and Ned is back leaning on the doorframe, all ears.

"You're not like any teacher I ever had before."

"What's your idea of a good teacher?"

"I had one in the sixth grade who was supposed to be the best in our school. He used to come up behind me and if I wasn't doing my work just the way he wanted it, he'd put his hand on the back of my head and bang my head on the desk top."

"Did you like that?"

"I don't know. No. I guess not. But he was a good teacher."

"You didn't learn very much though."

"That's true."

"I had a good teacher once, Mrs. B."

Everyone laughs. By this time no one is studying math, and even Matt has emerged from the kitchen hideaway to hear what's going on.

"What was good about that teacher?"

"She didn't give us a hard time the way you do, or tell us we were wrong about things. She was sweet and nice. I remember she used to say our answers were 'incomplete.' Never WRONG the way you do. She thought it was gloomy to talk about bad things, and I guess she thought everything was right in some way or other."

"Do you mean that you made mistakes because you didn't know enough?"

"Something like that. She'd say we hadn't gone quite far enough or it was something that could be completed."

"That's not bad. Aristotle said if you knew enough, you'd hit the mark."

"I think it's confusing. You couldn't tell right from wrong."

"Yeah, I'll admit I didn't like it so much. But she was nice to me."

"Getting back to Franny. I think it's wrong to do a lot of work for the sake of industry. It's different if work leads to an increase in knowledge or skill."

"Maybe so. But I still say the student does the work and the teacher marks it. The student's job is to do what the teacher tells him, and that's all. You can't blast Franny for doing what you or the book tells her to do."

"Right. And if she gets a lot wrong, she still gets credit for doing the work."

"Well, if that's your idea of school, you ought to be getting ready to change it."

"Why should we?"

"Because you've failed in schools like that—or schools you thought were like that."

"Leave it to Buzzard Heinemann to rub it in."

"Ned! In the doorway again?"

"I can't study."

"You're impossible. Anyway, you've had your chance to study by yourself, and you didn't. So come on all the way in and sit down with the rest of us."

"Mrs. Bernstein, what's the use of this crappy algebra?"

"Yeah. Why do we have to study it?"

"My father says you learn useful things in school. But I can't see how that goes for algebra. He doesn't use it. Why study things you can't use?"

"What does 'useful' mean?"

"It'll get you somewhere. Help you earn more money. Use it, you know."

"Practical."

"Start a discussion like this, and old Buz will give us a lecture."

"I'm afraid you're in for it. You like to solve puzzles and riddles, don't you?"

"Sometimes."

"It's natural. You would have the same pleasure solving algebra problems if you didn't have so many explosive mines planted around the classroom. If you didn't have to learn it, for instance, you'd probably want to. But it's not just fun, either. Math challenges your power to reason, and as you apply yourself to it your mind expands. When you learn more math or poetry, Latin or history, your internal life becomes more textured and interesting. In my opinion that's your chance to become more human. I'd say that we study to become more ourselves, more active as reasonable human beings."

"OK. I'll take your word for it, Buz."

"Are you gonna correct my work now, Mrs. B?"

"He sounds like a real teacher when he gets going like that, doesn't he?"

I know how little chance we have of convincing these students to substitute the intellectual values of education for the practicality of training. They have to prepare themselves for jobs and a place in society. It is true that in a sense they are rebelling against the system, but they are not consciously opposed to the idea that society is a market place which they are preparing to enter with a powerful acquisitiveness for goods and status. They have only become suspicious of the vague ideals that have been grafted onto this view, which to them do not constitute ultimate goals but are the ritual decoration of an otherwise grim and cynical utilitarianism. Besides being so self-preoccupied, they hardly formulate for themselves a goal of bettering society as a dwelling for the spirit.

We find that students with learning problems especially identify knowledge and formal school learning with the familiar process by which all values become tools for getting somewhere or owning something. They suffer from feeling pushed around and manipulated by their elders and thus converted into commodities, too. We want to show them that they will gain integrity when they value their own development as men and respect a similar development in others. We wish we knew how to reconcile the material demands of modern society with the need for spiritual development. We do not have more than the vague outlines of a creed; yet we can deal with specific issues clearly and consistently. For example, when Matt raises the question of drugs like peyote, we know our stand. We will discuss it privately with him but we

affirm that whatever robs man of his reason or impairs it or distorts his judgment in the name of exploration and sensation takes
something away from him as a man. No "scientism" disguises
the inevitable destructiveness to self-sovereignty. We tell Matt
that if he experiments with drugs after being informed of their
evil effects, we will no longer work with him because he will be
violating the principles of growth and independence upon which
all our work stands. Matt considers all this as seriously as we present it, and even though he has not yet decided on a course of
action, he seems relieved by our determined opposition.

Ned's problems, too, are all unresolved. His day has been a total
loss academically because he has been too nervous and distracted
to concentrate on school work. He has refused to discuss it, and
we have allowed him freedom to find his own way out. However,
he has only become more fidgety, discovering that being "let
alone" is the last thing he wants. The intense discussions and the
joking of the others beckon him back into the group.

"Well, Ned. Let's have it. What's going on with you?"

"What do you mean?"

"What's wrong?"

"Oh, you mean about my studying?"

"Right."

"Well, I tried to work, but I couldn't concentrate. You know
that."

"Yes, but I don't know why."

"I don't either. It's just one of those things."

"No, Ned. That won't get by."

"If I don't know why, I don't know. What do you want, blood?"

"I believe you know something about what is making you so
jittery. Can't you tell us?"

"I don't know."

"I've already said that's not acceptable."

"Well, that's tough shit."

"If you're angry you don't need to swear at me. You can just
say that you're angry."

"You're getting my ass!"

"Ned, say what you mean!"

"I mean you're trying to get me to talk. I don't have to."

"No, you don't have to. But you can't do schoolwork and if you won't talk about your feelings there is nothing for you to do here. You should go home."

"Go home? Are you out of your mind?"

"No. We're not offering you shelter from the cold. If you can't do anything today, you can go home and come back tomorrow to try again."

"I don't want to go home."

"Well then, try and tell us what's wrong with you today. Isn't that exactly why you're here—to find out what holds you up when you can't study?"

"I already told you I don't know."

"You may not know all about it, but you know something. I think if you told us what that something is we could find out more, together."

Ned's ready smile has long since vanished. His full lips are pouting and tears arise. He glares defiantly about him. Despite his sullen expression and the welling tears, his eyes flash fire. The others have stopped their work to listen intently and seriously. Ned's silence is eloquent and embarrassing.

"Come on, Ned. Mrs. Bernstein is certainly on your side. Say what's on your mind."

Ned remains silent.

"OK, Ned. I'm sorry, but you can't just sit there. If you have nothing to say, go. You can come back tomorrow and we'll discuss it then."

"No!"

Another crisis. We must stand our ground against his refusal and belligerence. My partner is now worried that Ned may choose violence as his way and push himself beyond the point where we can work with him at all. I fear shoving him out the door may lead to a scuffle, if things come to that. We cannot sidestep this clash of wills if we are ever to get to the bottom of his problems. This happens with nearly every boy who wants to know how far we will go. We are conscious of the risks, but close calls have never ended in a casualty. Students have been unable to go as deeply into their feelings and thoughts as we wanted, but none has walked out never to return on this account, nor has anyone ever struck us. All the same both of us are tense, for we never *know* what will happen.

"Ned, this is getting out of hand. You know we are going to enforce our rules. If you aren't going to abide by them we can't work with you."

"Ned, you're feeling pretty bad now, aren't you?"

"I sure am. Mrs. Bernstein is crowding me."

"Do you want to go on working with us?"

"Yes. Of course I do."

"Well, then you have to trust our judgment about what you are going to do. You've had every chance to work things out by yourself, and you couldn't. Now you need help, and even when you don't know just what it is, you can let us decide what is the best thing for you to do. You can accept our advice."

"What do you want me to do?"

"We want you to talk about what is keeping you from working. And if you can't do. that, we want you to leave quietly now and come back tomorrow to discuss the choice you made. There's no punishment. It's our way of recognizing that you can't do anything in school today."

"No punishment! Ha! I'll get the shaft at home. They'll say, 'What are you doing home now? Don't you know how much money we're spending to send you to that place?' Nag. Nag. Nag. Nag."

"You might be exaggerating their reaction. But I'll be glad to call up and explain our rules and procedures. I'm sure I can clear up some part of the problem."

"But, Ned, you don't have to go home. Why won't you talk about what's wrong?"

"If I told you what I thought, you'd get too sore. Look at Mr. Heinemann now. He's ready to bust a gut."

"He's not angry about what you're thinking or feeling. He's upset to think you can't give in on this point, after all the understanding and attention he's given you."

"You're right, Marilyn. I'd say his telling us now, when he's afraid to, and doesn't want to, would be a real giving for him, and a big step forward. I'm sure we can pretty much guarantee, Ned, that we won't be shocked or angered by your thoughts."

"Do you promise not to throw me out?"

"No. We can't promise that. You know us pretty well, though. Have we thrown anyone out yet?"

"No, but there's always a first time."

"Well, you'll have to take a chance. And at once, too. This is going on too long."

"No one's been thrown out for telling the truth, Ned. Some students have left because they couldn't ever tell us the real truth."

"What if I did go home?"

"Tomorrow we'd ask you why you chose to go home, so you'd still have to talk. You see—if you can't study, there's no escape. You'll have to talk."

"On with it for God's sake."

"Welllllluh. Remember the book I told you I was reading?"

"Yes. Some funny name."

"You don't listen to me very much. It was *The Palm-Wine Drinkard*."

"I recall that it's got some Surrealist effect. A man returns parts of his body to their owners and pays them rent, isn't it? Ugh!"

"I don't know. I haven't actually read it yet. I guess it's something like that."

"Come on, Ned. What's this book which you haven't read got to do with your being upset today?"

"You thought I had bought it, but I didn't. I saw it when I was browsing in a paperback bookstore, and I took it."

"You didn't pay for it?"

"No. Are you going to tell my parents and throw me out?"

"Why did you take it?"

"I wanted it."

"You have plenty of money. You could have paid for it."

"Two dollars? Why should I pay two dollars for a book? I only have $18 to last until Christmas."

"Oh, Ned. Not that again. If you wanted to buy a book I know your parents would be so delighted they'd surely give you the money for it."

"Not this month. They've told me they won't give me any more money for things I want."

"Can't you earn it?"

"That would be work."

"Well, however it is, Ned, you'll have to return it," says Marilyn, with so much sudden determination that I look at her in wonder. Believing that human existence is profoundly moral, we always take a clear stand on moral questions. Besides, we know our students expect and need a moral guidance that, as to specific matters at least, is unambiguous. Our plugs for personal responsibility in both the narrow sense of self and the wider context of society have caught their attention without so far persuading them, for instance, to stop being cruel or dishonest. They go on driving their cars recklessly and continue to violate those "minor" traffic laws that have deadly implications. Some do not pay debts; others keep things that do not belong to them. Tom smokes outside of school, though cigarettes threaten to kill him. Alden is faithless about appointments with his doctor and with his parents too. Jimmy does not return Tom's model engine, though we keep pressing him to do so. Unless their wrong deeds strongly and negatively influence their academic problems, we confine ourselves to comments and noises. Now Marilyn's tone implies a determination that Ned return his stolen book, and I am puzzled. It seems of minor importance compared with Matt's peyote. Drugs are so dangerous to the minds we are struggling to help that it is obvious we cannot tolerate any association with them. But stealing a paperback book is a common act, childish and wrong, but surely not often dangerous. However, Ned has dramatized this particular external problem and dragged it into school to stay. With book-stealing on his mind for whatever reason, he is too worried to study or learn in school. He challenges us to help him without giving us a choice of issues. He alone of the eight students wants to fight school responsibility in terms of an ethical question commonly dealt with outside school. We accept such a challenge because we can limit our interest to its application to school problems.

"No."

"I really mean it, Ned."

"I want to keep it. Are you going to tell them?"

"I don't know. That's not important. What is important is for you to decide to return it."

"Are you going to throw me out?"

"Not for stealing the book, no. But I am very clear that you must return it, or go back and pay for it."

"I don't see why I should."

"What upset you so today? Was it a bad conscience over stealing——," I say.

"Taking, Mr. Heinemann, taking. It's not big enough to call it stealing."

"You would have to quibble over that. It's stealing all right."

"I don't have a bad conscience over it. The owner will never miss it, and I needed it."

"So you were worried over what we would do?"

"Yes."

"I take it that means that we are important to you, and that even though you tell us how wrong we are about you, you want to stay with us."

"I wouldn't say 'want to.' I think it's better to say that I need you. I don't understand why because you're almost always wrong."

"At least we've come that far. I don't know what Mr. Heinemann thinks, but I know that I will work very hard to persuade you to return that book."

"What about my parents?"

"Ned, this is a matter that concerns you and us. I can see that if we should eventually part company we would have to explain to your parents why we failed with you. Then we might have to bring this matter up. But I'm sure it is not a question of telling them just to make you do what we want you to do. We want you to agree to return the book because you *see* it is the right thing for you to do."

"How are you ever going to do that?"

"We'll try."

"Ned, I think the reason you were upset about it and finally told us is that you want *us* to do something."

"Wrong again, Buz. You have a genius for being wrong."

Ned glares at me with that bitter anger reserved especially for me. Marilyn and he share a sympathetic understanding that I miss altogether. I have to labor to uncover what Marilyn has already sensed about this affair. Ned is not upset by a bad conscience. The

anxiety which kept him from studying stems from a serious intention to defy and defeat the growing influence of our work. This
very moment he is aglow with that spite and toughness which has
been so powerful within him. He tells us about the book to flaunt
his infantile willfulness and his "existential" freedom, challenging
us to stop him. It is a sign of his high intelligence that he knows
instinctively the seamlessness of responsibility. What he cannot
evade in our school he can destroy outside it. If he can threaten it
without arousing our full resistance, he will have found our weaknesses, our moral and intellectual cracks. He knows we cannot
really make him return the book, but he fears very much that we
can make him want to. He tells his story and pits his will against
ours, anxiously watching to see whether we will go all the way. He
is confused because he wants us to be stronger, and at the same
time hopes to keep his own willfulness intact. Either we insist on
the return of the book or we lose the possibility of his respect and
confidence. He will smile maliciously and wallow in an unattached
and floating existence.

"Aren't you going to punish him?" demands Jimmy, indignantly.
He is enchanted by the revelation and his face is flushed in anticipation of an exciting climax.

"Aren't you even going to blast him?"

"We're going to try to get him to return the book."

"What a crazy school!"

"Yeah," comments Matt, "I should think this story was worth
a laugh, anyway! Imagine Ned sneaking a book he probably can't
read out of a store, and getting away with it. You didn't even
smile!"

"It's not funny, Matt. What Ned did was really sad because it
shows that he is still so far back in his childhood that he takes
things from others in a completely selfish way without considering
their needs."

"Ned is punishing himself, isn't he? He's lost the whole day as
far as schoolwork goes."

"There they go, trying to make a big deal out of it. You teachers are really square. Taking that book is strong, not weak!"

"Is that why you were so calm, collected, and efficient today?"

"On Target! But I think I would have been OK if Mrs. B had corrected my work when I wanted her to."

"Are you still angry about that?"

"Not angry. Just irritated."

"You're full of it, Ned."

"I'm going to say it again and again, Ned. What you did was wrong, and you must return the book. But meanwhile I *will* correct your math work and you can then go ahead with your homework tonight."

"OK, everyone. Time for composition writing," calls Mrs. Hunt.

The class ends with the assignment of homework. We would like it if Franny would not take any, but she demands it for fear of her mother's questions if she comes home without schoolwork, and she still thinks industry will appease the Gods of Education. On the other hand, Ned, who evades it, needs regularly assigned tasks which he accepts with a show of anger. The faint stirrings of conscience may be there; we risk its total loss if we do not require him to develop it and to drop his increasingly conscious infantilism.

VI ❧ *What Am I?*

OPEN A BOOK for a fact or an idea, and someone says, "Ouch!", suspending subject matter while he looks reluctantly at the inner obstruction and feels his way around it. Openly refusing to "absorb," he does take time to think and argue. No sooner are things cleared up for a return to the subject, when someone else shouts, "Whoa! Not me!"

Progress through Algebra I or the *Lord of the Flies* is creeping at a petty pace, as it seems, when the day comes to write reports. These are sent to parents and describe the learning blocks and how the students are dealing with them. The reports do not focus attention on hoped-for advances in the mastery of subjects or skills, though students do unearth unsuspected achievements long buried under fear and resentment. Those who at first thought our attitude toward schoolwork soft now begin to realize how exacting it can be to achieve the self-knowledge students must acquire and learn to express while still struggling with academic subjects.

Nevertheless, schools eventually taking our students will look for the kind of evidence of progress that can be measured quantitatively; and parents prefer these seemingly accurate data, too. To meet this practical need, we use standardized tests yielding scores which rank students within nationally selected groupings. The students hate and fear these multiple-choice tests which, in our opinion, measure ability to perform mimetically and efficiently more accurately than learning achievements. Antithetical to the creative aims of education, these tests are nevertheless so firmly planted in the educational landscape that all students must master the techniques of doing well on them.

The appearance of familiar forms of Cooperative and Stanford Achievement tests on the oval table opens the floodgates of re-

sentment which the students hope will wash out the planned testing, or, at the very least, spoil the regimentation needed for an
orderly administration of the tests.

We seek to quiet their fears by interpreting them and by explaining the limited purposes of the tests. We try to lower the
charge on the expectations of failure by making current test success seem less urgent. After discussion, all but Alden and Matt re-
sign themselves to being tested. This passivity is very different, of
course, from any resolution to take tests.

Alden demands to be allowed to go home, and Matt threatens
to do so. For the first time we forbid Alden to leave, while urging
Matt to carry out his threats. Jimmy explodes at our unfairness.

"What is this?" Jimmy demands. "I want to study by myself,
and Alden wants to go home, and you say no. We have to take
the tests! But not Matt. He can leave if he wants to! Is that
justice?"

"Yes, it is. It would be unjust to treat you as if you were all the
same. Matt has yet to walk out of here. He's trying to keep alive
the fiction that he's being forced to stay so he can rage on against
us. But you two have never had any qualms about ditching school
when you felt like it. So it's different."

"Look! My glasses won't stay on," Matt complains. "Now how
can I take the tests?"

"Leave, if you want to. Just shut up and leave—or stay and
listen. I want everyone to be quiet so I can explain about the
tests."

"I would leave if I didn't think you'd get back at me for it."

"Back at you! What an idea! How would you damage me by
leaving?"

"I'd leave because these children are—well, I can't say it."

"Say it!"

"Oh, Matt. Get up the nerve to go. It would be a relief to all of
us to see that you actually did do something you wanted to."

"Hah!"

"Say, Tom, what are you doing hiding behind that wall of
books? You ought to listen closely to what I say."

"He's trying to fold a piece of Kleenex into a closed box that
will stand up by itself."

"It's impossible. He can't do it."

"Tom put that away, and put aside your wall. I'm not attacking you."

"I can't. Matt bet me $10 that I couldn't make the Kleenex box stand up."

"Did you, Matt?"

"Yes, I did. I can't help it if he's such a little fool."

"Matt, this is getting terrible. You are just sneaky and devious. Trying to control Tom and break up the testing at the same time. If there's a way to act like a stinker you'll find it! Why can't you just refuse to take the tests and walk out on them?"

"That's what you'd like me to do, isn't it?"

"I'm not trying to get you to do that, if that's what you mean. I wish you'd stay and take a positive attitude toward the work. But you're boiling inside, and you don't dare express it openly. I'd rather see you slam out of here in a rage than have you manipulate others to vent your feelings."

"You know how I hate to be here, and what a mistake I think it was for me to have come in the first place."

"That's not what I mean, Matt. I don't think it's been a mistake at all. Quite the reverse. Next to your shrinker it's the most important positive step you've taken for a long time. But you have to convince yourself that you are actually coming here of your own choice and not because we have any power to make you."

"It's disgusting!"

"So go!"

"Maybe it's because the tests bug me. Today you're making RSS like the old Academy, and all those old feelings come roaring up. I just can't help getting furious."

Matt's insight, spoken aloud, reflects what the rest feel. Bringing a temporary reassurance and a brief calm to the room, it allows us to give the necessary instructions about the tests. When we start administering them, we keep a businesslike atmosphere as long as the gathering storm permits. The disturbances tests generate are not going to submit to inner controls until much later in the year.

At first sight our group seems to be bending quietly over their test booklets. They look studious, diligent. Close inspection dispells the illusion. Jimmy's face is beet-red, but not from the effort of concentrating. He is seething with emotion. Tom slowly shakes his head, and clucks quietly. Ned and Matt look more absorbed, but when I peer over Matt's shoulder, I find him defiantly working backward from the last problem in the booklet toward the first. Ned is writing in answers so fast that they must be random guesses. Alden's throat rumbles, and I dart over. He has covered the open page of his booklet with the word SHIT, but he bends over a problem when he sees me. I motion to him to keep going, and move to look over Franny's shoulder. She is self-contained and tense, but to judge from her flushed face she, like Jimmy, is stewing. Amy is attacking her fingernails with savagery, and frequently looks around the room. Marilyn and I try to do justice to the requirements of test administration. It is not easy for us to watch their tensions build up without stepping in to offer some sort of relief. However, one word of special recognition or sympathy would shatter the fragile order. The demand for disciplined behavior and uninterrupted production is a reminder of the realities of normal school life and will ultimately contribute to an improved morale.

At last Alden explodes. His staccato yelps follow scrape of chair and shuffle of feet. Jimmy's face looks apoplectic, but Alden's is black with rage. He has jumped to his feet and is tearing his test booklet to shreds, crumpling and strewing the pieces all over. Marilyn is earnestly talking to him to maintain what order she can.

"It's all right, Alden. Keep it quiet. The others have to have their chance to work. Let's go into the kitchen to discuss it."

"Can I smoke?"

"Yes. But just get in there. Hop!"

Matt looks up and mutters something about smoking, gazing enviously at Alden's retreating figure. Marilyn's quick action keeps the tests going. We'll surely be able to finish the first section and have our break. Marilyn, accompanying Alden, talks to him in a steady, quiet tone which seems to help him keep control of himself.

"Time's up. Stop work. Halt! Everyone."

"Whewewewew," Jimmy whistles the air out of his system.

"Thank God! I'm sure glad that's over. Gimme a cigarette, Jimmy, will you?"

"Sure, Matt. Gotta match?"

"Yeah. Thanks."

"I'm doing better this time, I think. How much more will there be today?"

"Another hour, Amy."

"What's happening to Alden? Is he going home?" asks Franny.

"Not yet. We're going to talk with him when you go back to the tests."

"I'll bet he rams out of here," says Jimmy. "But don't start talking about him now. He's boring."

"I'll say," agrees Matt, who after the strain of the tests shows more friendliness for Jimmy than he ever did before. "Now, would you like me to explain about what is really important? The realm of abstract generalities!"

"No!" Jimmy yells. "That's even more boring, Nut!"

"Bourgeois bastard!" Matt roars in a wrathful voice we have never heard before.

We all turn to see what is happening, for Matt is pounding the table cursing Jimmy roundly. His dark eyes are flashing and his body is tense and vigorous. "What oafish brats you all are. And clumsy Mama Bernstein from the Bronx and creepiest of all, Pops Heinemann from the Nasalwest! Fools! What am I doing among you? I hate you all! I'm getting out of here!" Matt jumps up and rushes out, slamming the door so hard the house shakes.

"Well," exclaims Marilyn, "what brought that on?"

"I don't know exactly. Something Jimmy said. But it's been coming."

"What a relief! I thought he'd never have the courage to get angry like that!"

"What do you mean by that?" asks Amy.

"Matt is really afraid of the force of his own fury. Maybe he's even angrier than we think. Perhaps he ought to be afraid."

"No matter how he spreads his anger, Bob, I always get the brunt. That's why I've been hoping he'd open up. I think I feel it twice as much as you do because it's directed against females, particularly me, with at least twice the force he uses on men."

"Well, this certainly clears the air."

"Will he come back do you think? He seemed pretty sore to me."

"I think he will. In fact I'm sure of it. He has to find out whether his explosion was harmless or not."

"Are you going to make him take the tests later?"

"No. He's taken a much more important test right now than the thing on paper would be."

"You mean the test of his own anger?"

"Partly. But not only that. Now he can find out whether he is really free to come and go. He'll never be able to study as long as he can blame someone for making him be in school."

"OK. It's time to get back to testing. Bob, after we get them settled please come in with me to talk with Alden. He's still upset, and all I've been able to do is keep him from rushing out the door."

A change in the mood of the others gives me a chance. They begin the next section of tests easily. Matt has gone, and resistance is decreased. Their energies have been consumed in emotional responses, and the lull in tension betokens fatigue and resignation. They do not concentrate well, but they are docile about going through the motions while I leave them for the kitchen.

"What happened, Alden?"

"I told Mrs. Bernstein. I can't do these tests."

"I guess we know that, Alden. But we want you to make a beginning. Someday you have to start the school things you 'can't' do."

"Aren't you going to punish me for tearing up the test?"

"No. It was an honest thing to do and no great loss. The booklets are pretty inexpensive to buy. I don't even mind your writing dirty words all over the pages. You acted openly when you were angry. You're still here and talking so actually I'm pleased with you."

"Why *are* you so angry about the tests, Alden? It must be more than just feeling unable to do them."

"I think I better go home now."

"Why?"

"I wanted to go before, but you wouldn't let me."

"Well, you can go now. But I don't want you to."

"I tried your crappy old tests for you. Now I want to go home."

"What is the reason?"

"I feel like it."

"You can do math or something, instead of the tests."

"No."

"Tell us why."

His silence stretches out. He looks out the window then at the floor.

"What happened, Alden. Tell me!"

His mouth is set, and he makes a turning gesture with his hand.

"You can't just sulk like that, Alden. It's what you do every time we insist on knowing what's bothering you. But the time for that is past. I won't take it any more. You treat me with the same sullen silence you turn on your father when he puts on the pressure. But I'm not your father. Mrs. Bernstein and I are your friends, and you ought to treat us like friends—not members of the family."

Alden looks at us now, clenching his fists. He still says nothing.

"I agree with you, Bob. This is it. Yesterday he admitted that he thought we were really on his side. But today, because he 'feels like it' he is ready to cancel out our friendship. We can't go on like that."

"Click! Click! I've turned you off."

"Give, Alden. Give. And now!"

"Why should I?"

"Because we are asking you to."

"So what?"

"That's part of friendship, Alden. It can't be a one way street where we do all the giving. You have to offer something, too."

"Well . . . Now, don't get sore!"

"About what? We're already sore about your attitude."

"I mean about what's bothering me."

"Just tell us without all the padding."

"You would! OK, I'll tell. But you'll pay for making me do something I don't want to do. OK, OK, don't flip your wig. It's my parents' plan for the Christmas Vacation."

"We know about that. You told us yesterday. They want to

take a couple of extra days because they are going to Florida, and we told you not to come back here even one day late, anyway."

"I told them what you said."

"Why should that upset you so? We didn't want Jimmy to take long weekends to please his parents, and we objected to Matt's making his doctor appointments during school hours, and you saw the point. You said you wanted to be back here on time."

"I do. And I told them that, too. I told them I'd come back myself. They didn't believe me. They figured I was plotting to break up *their* vacation, and they didn't believe you wouldn't let me come in late. Anyway, my mother thinks I'm too young to travel alone. I feel lousy."

"Is your father suspicious of you, too?"

"I don't know. But it doesn't matter what you say. I want to get out of here."

"Why?"

"Why? Why, again! I don't know. I just do!"

"Leave the matches alone, Alden. Don't start playing with fire now. It's absolutely outlawed on these premises. Work it out with your psychiatrist, not here."

"You never did tell me what playing with matches is supposed to be a sign of, Mr. Heinemann. One of your ideas about sex, probably."

"Don't start off in that direction with him, Bob. Let's get back to the subject. About why you want to go, Alden. Tell us."

"Do you want to leave early today as a kind of revenge because we persuaded you to give up a couple of days in Florida at Christmas?"

"Click! I turned you off way back."

"You'll have to turn me back on. Leave now if you want to. But if you go now without explaining why, I for one want to talk about whether we should take you back."

"Alden, what will you do if you go now?"

"I'll drive around for a while. Then I'll go in town and buy some records and go home and play them. Why are you looking like that? I'll have fun."

"I worry about what you are doing now. You're far too angry to drive around safely. If you are so upset you can't stay in school,

I'm afraid of what might happen to you or to someone else with you behind the wheel. But it's very sad that you want to go out and buy something instead of coming to grips with whatever is wrong."

"Why don't you walk down to the square, Alden. Maybe you'll cool off a little. Come back afterward and either discuss it or do some schoolwork. Maybe it's mostly the testing that's got your goat."

"No, Bob. I think this is too serious. He can't just turn us off with his 'I don't knows' and 'I don't cares.' Not after all we've been through with him. You nursed him along until he felt strong enough to come to school on a regular schedule. He's willing to let me help him when he wants to get a bigger allowance from his father, or when he gets mixed up in his work, or when he feels lost and alone and wants me to care about it. I'm just not going to let him treat me like that. I want him to tell me why he's in such a hurry to get out of here today. If he can't give on that point, I don't see how I can go on working with him."

"See. You're threatening now. You always claim you don't threaten us, but you do."

"It's not a threat, Alden. Mrs. Bernstein is stating a fact. She doesn't mean that she wants to punish you by not working with you. Hasn't she taken just about all the crap you had to give? Why should she suddenly turn on you and take revenge for this affair?"

"I've given her plenty of bad times, I guess . . ."

"Well, she's just stating the plain truth that if you can't ever give to us when we ask you to and think you should, there is no trust and no mutuality in our relationship. And then we are really unable to help you."

"That's true. I do want to go on working with you, Alden, but if there's no chance of your accepting responsibility here, it would be much better to recognize the situation. After all, you may be able to find your answers somewhere else."

"This is the end of the line for me, Mrs. B. Last Chance Academy. And you are making a threat," Alden mutters, his expression still darkening.

"You can't think every statement we make telling you how we

deal with problems is a threat, at least in the sense that we are dangling it over your head to get you to do what we want. It's ridiculous. It's like saying it's a threat to tell you that you'll get cold if you go without your clothes in the winter."

"Call it what you will, Alden. Let's get on with it. We've left the others testing in there to concentrate on you and your problems. But we can't do it all day. They need us, too."

"I've got it, Alden. I think the reason you're so angry is that your parents don't think you're mature enough to travel alone. Is that it?"

"SHUT UP."

"Getting furious enough to leave school, going out to buy yourself some records and going home to play them! Is that supposed to show how mature you are?"

"SHUT UP."

"If I'm on the right track I won't stop now."

"You're on the right track."

"Do you want to grow up, Alden?"

"I'm old enough to go on the train or plane by myself."

"That's not an answer to my question. The way things are going, twenty or thirty years from now you'll be living in that little old cottage on the family acres. I see you now, counting your trust fund in the glow of the sunset. You've got it made in the shade. Why should you grow up? Peter Pan rides again!"

"Oh, you're so funny, Mr. Heinemann. Not! I have time to change. Anyway there isn't any trust fund. Well, maybe just a small one."

"Would you like us to talk to your parents for you? Mr. Heinemann can call up and explain our point of view about the vacation. We think you're old enough to travel alone, and we'd be glad to say so. Or we can discuss it with them when we have our conference all together."

"No. Never. Don't say a thing to them about it."

"Well then. Stay now and do some schoolwork. You can skip the tests for today."

"Let him write a composition now. About his feelings today."

"I still want to go home. I need to. I have to tell my mother something."

"You can telephone her. If you leave now, you'll lose one more chance to change. Don't do that to yourself."

"Alden, think of it this way. If you stay now, when you want to follow an impulse to go out and buy, and if you can settle down to some work, you'll be showing all of us—including your parents—that you are beginning to grow up."

"Pretty sneaky, Mr. Buz. But you're getting that look, too, Mrs. B. OK. I'll try it."

"Good. Good for you. Write."

"What'll I write about?"

"Oh . . . the whole question of your urges to be always a child like Peter Pan. Or why you think you can travel alone. Anything that means something to you."

"I'm pleased with you now, Alden. Not only for giving something, but for wanting to stay in school. Cutting short a vacation just to be in school would have been unthinkable two months ago, wouldn't it?"

"God, yes! What are you two doing to me?"

"Big error, Marilyn. Praising him is like asking to be hit."

"You're right, Buz. Which reminds me, Mrs. B. Have you been eating my tuna-fish sandwiches lately?"

"Yes, when you've abandoned them."

"I thought so. You're looking a bit plumper these days."

"Ouch!"

"Look, why don't you and Mr. Heinemann go back to the others now? Then I can write. Boy, am I going to blast my parents in this installment!"

The fruits of independence suddenly attract Alden. Our heavy insistence coming at such a moment helps him consciously link a school commitment to self-gratification. It also tickles his fancy to accept academic obligations as a way to thwart his parents. They have long worn an air of contempt for school which he has with justification interpreted as a license to stay uncommitted. To claim that his parents promote his academic lapses is not as paradoxical as it seems, when their unconscious drives are taken into account.

How much we would like to sniff around and follow some of the leads that stare us in the face! We would like to ask Alden why his parents, who think him too irresponsible to travel alone, give him a car to drive! We want to ask whether his parents' attitude toward the importance of school does not show a marked change when school interferes with *their* pleasures, or even whether his outrageous behavior in school is not an acting-out of their unconscious wishes. He is not ready for insights of this order and we will not push for them. They are better explored in his psychotherapy.

Family preoccupations are always seething, but the tests bring on further storms of conflict. Wild hope for perfect scores soars within their hearts; yet premonitions of total failure possess them. The test is that dread moment when the student faces alone the full power of the teacher, when weakness may flood into disaster. Often those who should have foreseen this result are irrational about it and suppose that the test will magically prove that all the "little troubles" in the classroom are false alarms. Over and over again they have been wretchedly disappointed. Little wonder that they refuse now to follow instructions or that they do their work backward and give up! Only a series of confrontations accompanied by crises, discussions, and changes in attitudes will make it possible for these students to concentrate on problem solving when they take tests.

After an absence of several days, Matt returns to school without urging; Alden stays in school for more full days than before; Ned's confession of thievery opens for serious discussion issues related to existential expediency and ethical principles. Yet, as the students move closer to confidence in us, they become meaner, more vicious. Each tries to shoot down our resolution, our sense of right, testing our willingness to go out on those limbs which appear most dangerous. Perhaps it seems an extra weakness in him that he cannot learn without close personal confidence in adults. Many students in regular school strive and succeed all the more efficiently in an atmosphere of thinly veiled dishonesty, mistrust, and selfishness. Not ours. Matt, Ned, Alden—in fact every one of them—have had their trust crushed by betrayal and disappointment. The wounds are so deep that the revival and healing of belief are indispensable to eventual academic recovery, and will give their personalities depths of compassion and understanding denied to their less sensitive, though perhaps more fortunate fellows.

The coming of reports and parents' conferences briefly but seriously disrupts the growth of this trust, rekindling ancient suspicions of adult plots and maneuvers. The students learning to be truthful with us are still afraid to be open with their parents and expect us to get them into trouble because we know "too much," or because, used to talking one way at home and another in school, they may be "caught out." They anticipate revenge and punishment and are altogether incredulous of "good" results.

An important step toward meeting their fears is to insist that students read written reports before they are mailed to their parents. Many classroom discussions about the aims of the conferences as well as relevant characteristics of individuals help worried students understand how their personal problems can be conceptually formulated and rationally discussed, even by themselves. They are reassured by the discovery that some problems are shared; yet they also like to know which of their qualities are really individual and less widely distributed in the group. Our students are eager for an honest appraisal of themselves; answering the question "What Am I?" alleviates some of the anxiety about reporting.

It is especially important to deal directly with Matt, whose parents are too remote.

"Let's start with concentration, Matt," we say. "Your mind is seldom held by the logical development of material. Left alone, you turn to watch your private movies or daydreams. In a group you watch us, suspicious that one of us is sneaking about to get some kind of control over you. You are not curious enough about the outside world. Of course, you may have been once, but now your reflex is to 'socialize' any learning. For instance, if you answer a question the only reason you try for a right answer is to secure *social* notice."

"Doesn't everyone work for approval and recognition?"

"Of course, but not *exclusively*, as you seem to do. Your interest is shallow, your learning flimsy. Emphasis on the social rewards of learning, however common, tends to confuse social conformity with truth and knowledge, with *really* being right. You equate disciplined learning with middle-class, practical, getting-ahead, money-making goals. You strike an upper-class attitude of already *having* the money and wanting to 'enjoy'; you pursue ideas—not to organize your world, or to follow an interest, but because they *sound* good. It's the sound that helps you 'belong.' "

"Do you mean my ideas about dividing the world into the Realm of Abstract Generalities versus the Realm of Material things, ROMT?"

"Exactly. When you explain it, you get tangled up in more generalities. Your thinking is pretentious and vague, but since it *sounds* abstract you are satisfied. That sound is, like conspicuous consumption, a showy signal of upper-class money and leisure time."

"What's that got to do with learning problems?"

"You turn away from the rational. Your 'ideas' form superstructures without foundations. You are simply pasting bits of echoes together to make your 'sound.' You turn scornful when asked to dig in and analyze. Meticulous inquiries suggest to you a trap leading to a plodding, bourgeois life. Actually, the more unproductive your ideas are, the more stubbornly you hold them; some class horror makes you abandon common sense. The obvious is 'bourgeois,' so you seek the esoteric. Teaching you, making your mind work in a disciplined way with details and routines building up to real insights and genuine abstractions, makes you furious, for you are aware that going deeply into a subject would get you psychologically involved. You'd lose the precious prerogative of willfulness. In short, you oppose honest intellectual labor, and your learning problems are still serious."

Franny offers the other side of Matt's bourgeois coin. Knowing the right answers has a weighted social meaning for her, too, but *her* ambition is for that perfection of detail which cloaks a strong fear of general ideas. For her, learning is an accounting process in which details are labeled and arranged. Bearing down exclusively on the concrete, she inhibits the formation of concepts and suppresses the quickness of mind and feeling that would normally flow. Reading thus becomes a memorization process nearly devoid of associative thought. The pressure of time limits to which students are normally subjected when studying causes her to panic, for she dares not rely on reason and intuition. Franny's conscientiousness is excessive because she turns to it alone for self-defense. She can always say that she tries.

Jimmy's biggest worry about reports is that they will itemize his daily misdemeanors. He approaches the letter to his parents as if it were to be a court calendar:

Dear Mr. and Mrs. Stevens,

"As we have been in close contact throughout this period, we can summarize the results of Jimmy's work here.

"He came to RSS to find a remedy for his poor performance in public school. Soon after we began together, it was clear Jimmy was not suffering from a specific learning disability. The trouble seemed to lie in general disaffection with school and even the aims of education. Jimmy not only had no personal commitment whatever to school learning, but he was already seriously considering a total exclusion of such responsibility from his future life. However, he began balancing this total rejection against the long-range consequences which with his intelligent common sense he easily discerned; ditching school does not seem the perfect answer to his school problems when doing so might cut him off from future material advantages. It is a big step forward that he is now trying to reconcile these opposing tendencies.

"This has proven a more difficult task than it seemed because Jimmy stalls over the question of authority. To follow the directions of the teacher, even those given in print, means a personal submission which he cannot yet endure.

"Of course this has been a basic problem from the outset, but Jimmy has been making headway with it, responding affirmatively to the personal feelings he is developing for us. He devotes much energy to keeping separate his feelings about us as friends from those aroused when we instruct. When he sees us as teachers, he still reaches out for those disruptive teen-age alliances. But sometimes our friendship reassures him, and he seeks our help.

"Jimmy conceives of most school subjects as devices used by adults to control and manipulate him. Unquestionably earlier experiences elsewhere led him to reject the road of academic knowledge as an acceptable path toward maturity and independence.

"Jimmy's major effort now is to be conscious about joining his two worlds, to accept school as a place where an interest vital to his whole life can be developed. It takes a long time to convince him that our academic program is not a screen behind which we are scheming for domination. We think he is beginning to share our view that through academic learning he may convert his narrow world into a larger and more creative one.

"Jimmy took a series of standardized tests last week, and the results may be compared with those he took in September. They seem to indicate progress all along the line. We report on the English achievement scores below:*

	Percentile September	Percentile December
Vocabulary	87	84
Speed of comprehension	—1	67
Level of comprehension	4	89
Total reading	14	82
Mechanics of expression	20	46
Effectiveness of expression	33	47
Total English	17	74

* The scores are given as percentile for the end of the ninth grade in public schools.

"We now face clearly defined problems with Jimmy. The fact that he may want to do schoolwork and may like and trust us will not automatically remove difficulties. It is a beginning. He has shown that he can give of himself to others and that he can assume obligations in his work at RSS, but he continues willfully to assert his right and intention to reject these obligations unless the content of the subject matter and the conditions of the requirements please him. Also his motivation is too newly acquired to bring a sudden end to the distractability of his mind. His need to train his ears on all conversations in his vicinity and his inclination to avoid solitude continue to interfere with his concentration. Anticipating these difficulties should not in any way detract from a recognition of Jimmy's gains. He is doing an excellent job.

"We hope this report will serve as a jumping-off point for discussion with you. We look forward to meeting you again. Will next Wednesday at 7:30 be convenient?"

Each student is present to participate in his parent-school conference, after strong reaction against the idea when we first mention it. Some, like Tom, are so unaccustomed to rational argument that they fear open clashes between their parents and us will be physically explosive. All are conscious of certain differences and dread the meetings because they may have to choose sides. But probably the most serious student resistance is based on the objection that joint conferences make the students also responsible for decisions. In more conventional parent-teacher meetings, where the student is "spared," only the adults are committed to a course of action while the failing student remains detached, quite free—he thinks—to do as he likes.

Persuading students and parents together to view rationally problems until now either ignored or smothered by emotional outbursts, requires boundless tact. We are not always capable of it, and the joint conferences sometimes misfire. All the same, it is the only way of dealing with parents consistent with our aim of inducing the student to become responsible for himself.

Jimmy now understands our major concern is for the "idea" of his problems. We count on his courage, understanding, and will to help himself.

"Good evening, Mr. and Mrs. Stevens. It's been a long time since we last saw each other. Hi, Jimmy. Thank goodness you came."

"Would I miss a discussion about me, Mrs. Bernstein?"

"I'm glad you're not going to miss this one."

"He said he was supposed to come," Mrs. Stevens says, smiling uncertainly. "We weren't sure whether to bring him or not."

"He's absolutely right, Mrs. Stevens. We've been working on him for weeks to make him come. He thinks we're going to sell him down the river tonight."

"Mmm—!" Mr. Stevens tries to be pleasant, but like many business executives shows a labored forbearance in the presence of educators, and is strained and impatient. Condescension will be our portion. We hope our patience will hold out.

"I know this is a somewhat unusual procedure, Mr. Stevens, but by now you know that our school is unusual anyway."

"We don't hear much about it from Jimmy. He doesn't seem to

have much work to do, but he isn't getting himself kicked out yet. So you must be doing him some good."

Jimmy's telltale blushes are coming on strong now because he has reported in considerable detail the numerous explosions his father has had over our homework policies.

"Don't think he hasn't given us a hard time, Mr. Stevens, but that's natural and that's the way we work."

"Yes, I appreciate that. Mmmmm—well, I suppose if he's here with us tonight you can't speak frankly as you would otherwise. Isn't that so?"

Jimmy still hovers as if he had accidentally stumbled into a family huddle about someone he didn't know. Mrs. Stevens hovers too, cringing before the blast of Mr. Stevens's aggressiveness. Mother and son are belligerently submissive, resentfully apologetic. Sitting stiffly, she looks up and glances around the room, and then down at the tabletop, as if gazing too long or moving too suddenly would cause an injury.

"No, Mr. Stevens. Quite the opposite. We've been almost brutally candid with Jimmy. Maybe you disapprove of our telling him so much. Some parents have thought we expect too much understanding from these kids. They often see their children as far weaker and more babyish than we do."

"I've been around a bit myself," replies Mr. Stevens, "and I know what these youngsters can think up. No, it isn't that. I just thought it'd be easier . . ."

"Well, it's really easier for us to talk everything out in front of him. Then we don't have to explain it all later. Anyway, I don't think we have anything to say about him that we haven't already said to him."

"Did he tell you that we gave him his report to read before we sent it home to you?"

"No, he didn't tell me."

"He told me, George," murmurs Mrs. Stevens, reddening and shrinking further into herself.

"Let's take the report as a starting point tonight. Did you have any questions about our views? Perhaps you think we've left out something or missed the boat somewhere."

"Oh, no," Mr. Stevens says. "Quite the contrary. You hit the nail on the head more than once." He takes the report from his pocket and studies the notes he has on the margins. "I agree that he can't stand most teachers, and that he can't move ahead until he shapes up. In fact I'm surprised that he doesn't seem to mind you people. I suppose that's a good sign."

"Doesn't the psychiatrist handle that part? I mean about his feelings," Mrs. Stevens blurts out.

"Now, Mother," Mr. Stevens is dealing with his wife. "Let these people talk. We want to hear what they have to say."

"Of course it must seem that the psychiatrist should do it. And I have no doubt that Jimmy's feelings about teachers are closely related to the emotional problems that he and his doctor work on. But however that may go, he has to work out those anti-teacher feelings with teachers, too."

"Well," exclaims Mr. Stevens, "things weren't handed to me that way. I did everything on my own. I had to work my way through college—and even take jobs after hours when I was in high school. And here's Jimmy with everything given to him." He pauses, but no one speaks. "I know this thing has emotional sides to it," he continues, feeling the effect of his own steamrollering. "That's why we're willing to pay for his going to the doctor." And now defiant again, "But, by God, sometimes I think he gets too much from us."

"Jimmy always seemed to need extra help," says Mrs. Stevens sadly, "I used to give it to him. When he was in grade school I'd go over his lessons with him every night—until he had them perfectly."

"Maybe you helped him too much, Mother," offers Mr. Stevens. "Could that be behind what you say in the report about his having to make up his mind to go on with school?"

"We don't know all the things that lie behind it. But he hasn't decided against getting an education yet. He just isn't sure about it."

"I'm the first one to say that a boy of his age couldn't know his own mind about a lot of things, but why can't he study anyway? Does he have to be so certain?"

"Yes, and the fact that you ask that backs up our idea about

Jimmy's being the kind of boy who has to mean it. He can't just go along as you say you've done."

"Why not?"

"After all you are his father, and I'm sure he ties this question of education in with his relationship to you. Sometimes boys who feel their parents put pressure on them to succeed in school become convinced that the only way they have to free themselves is to fail."

"I agree with you about that, Bob," Marilyn turns to me, "but I don't think it's the whole story. I think Jimmy has real doubts about his ability to do the work. This comes up all the time in algebra. When I set him up with problems that I know he can do, he stalls because he's afraid he can't do them by himself."

Mrs. Stevens looks at Marilyn with a kind of relief and nods her head in agreement. She understands many things about her son, but crises dumbfound her and she cannot get her thoughts out.

"There is a feeling of weakness in him that we don't seem to have much to do with," continues Marilyn, "and even though he's good about tackling his problems here, sometimes he's overwhelmed with self-doubts, and quits."

Mr. Stevens's nervousness increases, and his wife becomes distant again. The something incomplete in their son affects them deeply. Warning signals are hoisted and start to wave us off. Family secrets are beginning to surface. We are especially attentive to such signals because we want to sidestep skeletons. Even when parents want to trot them out we change the subject. They do not help us solve the school problems we are dealing with. We do not need confessions to be conscious of the human failings that beset all parents and children.

"Marilyn, building up his self-confidence is important. But all our students need help with that. I don't see how we can help him with it until he agrees to a personal commitment to school learning."

"I just wanted to bring this other question up because it complicates the whole problem. It makes it harder to commit yourself to something if you have real doubts about whether you can do it at all."

"If you want to talk about commitment," Mr. Stevens objects, "wasn't I committed to getting ahead and giving my future family the best of everything? That's why I worked hard in school. It's OK for guys to dig ditches if they can't do anything better. But when you've got drive and brains . . ."

"But you'd look down on Jimmy if he decided that digging ditches was for him," I break in.

"Oh, come on, Bob. Where would Jimmy get the energy to dig ditches? You know he'll settle for something easier."

"Let's ask him. Jimmy, you're here. What do you think you'd do?"

But Mr. Stevens continues, "I guess that's where we'll have to start, all right. I thought when he came here you'd straighten him out on that. What about the future, Son? What kind of job can you get when you haven't even finished high school—let alone college?"

This torrent of words shuts Jimmy off, and he reddens just as a horse lays back his ears, in stubborn refusal.

"Mr. Stevens, I think Jimmy really has something to say, though it is too hard for him to look that far ahead now."

"Well—" Jimmy begins, but looks down and stops.

"Come on, Jimmy. You've been learning how to say your thoughts. You do it in school—although I'll admit that sometimes you're just fooling us."

Jimmy smiles. Instead of resenting a reference to his deceitfulness, as I feared he might, he is proud of it. His father smiles, too, and now I remember Jimmy's story about stealing from an abandoned cottage near their summer place. The town constable had caught Jimmy rummaging around in the old house; and later his father roundly scolded him on the subject of thievery. The incident got its cutting edge for Jimmy when he saw his father prowl around a few nights later, carrying off a couple of chairs that appeared without explanation in the family "rec" room on the following day.

"Yeah, sometimes you and Mr. H will fall for anything."

"Right. But now let's have it. Tell us your thoughts about going on with school."

"My thoughts are kind of mixed up."

"Do you want to dig ditches all of your life?" Mr. Stevens demands.

"That really isn't the point, Mr. Stevens. There are so many things to be said first. Jimmy, can't we see what these thoughts are and try to clarify them a little?"

"I don't know where to start."

"Well—anywhere. You don't need to edit so much."

"Dad gets me so excited and then I can't seem to think what I want to."

"OK. But try now. That's what we're all here for—I mean to get a better idea of your problems."

"You can do it, Jimmy. You're good at it in school. C'mon."

"OK. Take my cousin—the one who's the foreman in the candy factory. He didn't finish high school, but he leads a great life. I think he has a ball."

"Do you think he has a better job than you could get if you became an engineer, say?"

"I mean he has a good time for himself. Nothing ever worries him. When he comes home from work, he's through. He relaxes and enjoys himself. Goes out and gets a beer, turns on the ball game. He doesn't worry about the Company the way Dad does."

"That's true, Son. I bring my job home with me. But don't forget your cousin John doesn't have any responsibilities to speak of. He doesn't have any children to look after or to plan for."

"What's wrong with that?" Jimmy demands belligerently. He is an artist with the serpent's tooth. His mother taps the floor with her toe, but continues to keep silent.

"Where would you be if your mother and I took that attitude?" snaps Mr. Stevens. Thunderbolts are in the air.

"See? I told you," Jimmy turns to Marilyn sneeringly. "How can you talk to him?"

"I think you can. I don't know what's stopping you unless you're afraid. You've talked to me about these things, and we often disagree."

"That's the way these two always go at each other," sighs Mrs. Stevens.

"He's been able to handle his feelings much better in school, Mrs. Stevens."

"Well, to tell the truth, he has at home, too. He talks much more directly and openly. Sometimes too much, I guess. I mean he talks right back to his father instead of turning away and going off as he used to do. At least sometimes."

"Why, Son, you know I'm on your side," Mr. Stevens makes another effort, but he can hardly disguise the satisfaction he feels over getting control of his son's feelings. "I get a little gruff when I have to wait for you to come around. I don't usually have to wait for what I want. Don't take your cousin as a model, boy. There's a lot about him you don't understand because you've never been told. John's never been able to stand on his own two feet. I've had to step in and pull him out of several jams. But we don't want to go into a lot of family stories here. That's not what we came all this way to discuss."

"OK. But it isn't just him. I can see he has his problems, too. It's that I'm not sure that I want your kind of life—with so much responsibility."

"Good, Jimmy. Now you're coming through. It's true, Mr. Stevens. Jimmy has a 'Thing,' as the kids say, about responsibility and being a teen-ager. He has the fantastic notion that the teen-ager's world is both immortal and free of nearly every obligation to the real adult world. Isn't that so, Jimmy?"

"Oh, I know I won't always be in my teens, but I see myself staying with a gang of kids, yes. I want to grow up to be on my own, and all like that, but I don't want to give up what you call 'Teeny' fun. You know, the music with the beat, and stuff like that."

"It's what he clings to with more devotion than anything else. He seems to find there the warm and comfortable feelings he wants."

"That's one of the reasons I sent him to your school, Mr. Heinemann. He was getting into trouble with those kids, as you know. But that's over now. He doesn't see the old gang so much any more. Do you, Jim, Son?"

"Well, no."

"Since that's taken care of I'd like to know why you aren't doing more schoolwork?"

"First of all, Mr. Stevens, it's not just a question of bad associates. He and Baa-Baa are still going steady. Jimmy still wraps himself up in pizza–twisting–teen-age cotton. He hasn't settled any part of the question of responsibility in an adult, real world. Taking on homework has this larger meaning now, and we don't assign it lightly. If he's not ready to do it, we won't give it to him."

"As far as getting into trouble goes, things are changing for Jimmy, Mr. Stevens. He still tries to get one or two of the boys to form a teen-age team against the teachers. But it's not the destructive behavior it used to be. The most serious thing he does is to cut school, but we see this as part of the school commitment problem—not as hoodlum behavior."

"Yes, that is real progress, Marilyn, but he still feels that teen-agers should make a group opposition to teachers in school."

"Well," smiles Mrs. Stevens, "I'm not too surprised to hear that. I remember feeling that way myself."

"You didn't like school, Mrs. Stevens?"

"Like it? Heavens no! I had quite a bit of trouble in school myself." Suddenly her eyes sparkle, "I wonder if that would have anything to do with Jimmy's attitude?"

"By now his feelings are a mixture of a lot of things, including that. But at RSS Jimmy has no reason to feel that way. I'm sure he knows he hasn't got to fight us. What do you say, Jimmy?"

"MMmmmmmmmmm."

"Oh please don't get coy now!"

"What does coy mean? . . . Never mind! I get it. I know you two want to find out what's right for me. But you *are* teachers, and that's what I can't stand."

"So, we know it's fun for you to fool us, and that makes you feel you have power over us no matter how school matters go."

"Yes. I get a kick out of it—getting you two to do what I plan for you."

"Jimmy!" his mother declares in a shocked voice.

"Don't stop him, Jane. He comes by that honestly, don't you think? I like to make people do what I want them to, too!"

"I'm glad you said that, Mr. Stevens, because Jimmy does really take after you—more than you think. He interprets the relationships between teachers and students as a struggle for power. As long as he thinks like that it's hard for him to get deeply interested in any school subject. He fights off interests that might be growing because he's afraid they'd interfere with his strategy."

"But why? Why does he see it that way?"

"Jimmy, you're the best person to answer your mother's question."

"If I do, I'll get creamed."

"By whom?"

"By . . . Well, never mind!"

"Son, if you think I'll punish you for spilling the beans, you're wrong. We're here to lay our cards out on the table."

"All right, then. My old teachers were out to get me. I know that. But that's not all. Remember those nights you tried to make me memorize all that stuff, Mom? Didn't the teachers put you up to it? They weren't about to let me have my fun. Things like that. And then Dad with his, 'Jim, Son,' always ordering me to get good grades—as if it was my fault that they gave me lousy ones! How does he know I'm not too stupid to learn the stuff? Half the time he treats me as if he thinks I am."

"Now, Son, nobody said you're stupid. Not at all. Maybe you're not college material but that's different."

"Yeah. Yeah!"

"It's true that he may not go to college, Mr. Stevens, but that will be out of choice—not because he isn't able. Jimmy is one of the most intelligent students we've had here. Have a good blush, Jimmy. I've wanted to get this in all evening. He learns very fast when his mind is on his work, and he can be awfully good at saying what he's learned, too, and putting it to use. There!"

"That's all very well, Mrs. Bernstein, but it won't fill up the bank account. When is he going to use it on schoolwork? As far as I can judge you don't get much done in class—with all the problems you have, if the others are like Jimmy. How will he be smart enough if he doesn't start studying now?"

"That's just the point, Mr. Stevens. He can't concentrate on school subjects until he's made his decision to continue formal education or give it up. When he makes his choice, and if it's in favor of school, as we hope, he's smart enough to make up for lost time easily. And he's learning quite a lot in school anyway. If we're not making much headway in math, we are in the reading."

"There's something to that. Jimmy doesn't say much about what he does in school, but when he says anything it's usually about a book you're reading with an awful name—something about flies. And the *Iliad*. He keeps mentioning Achilles, and he says 'By Zeus' instead of—well—unprintable things," Mrs. Stevens says.

"That's not what he used to say around here either," says Marilyn, smiling.

"Whoa! Mrs. B, that's enough."

"Jimmy can't really study now, and if we gave him assignments he'd probably make passes at doing them for the record, but his negative feelings would really deepen."

"The fact that he can't concentrate is a big problem."

"Why can't he?"

"For one thing he's always listening. He imagines that every conversation concerns him, and he keeps his ears open."

"I think there's another reason. One that we've already mentioned. He runs other people—or tries to. His friends, his teachers, anybody. He concentrates on that without much trouble."

"What do you say to that?"

"Well," he blushes deeply, and seems undecided whether to speak. "Well, maybe you're sort of right about that. But that's not the only thing."

"What do you mean?"

"Probably he means that he can't do the work because he's been away from real schoolwork for too long," breaks in his father. Jimmy's eyes shoot daggers.

"Possibly, Mr. Stevens, but I don't think that's what Jimmy was going to say. I'd like to hear him out. What he can contribute to our discussion will be the most valuable part of it."

No one speaks. Jimmy struggles with himself. Silence is excruciating to most adults, but unbearable for adolescents.

"What bothers me sometimes is that I'm thinking a lot about things that happen at home. I get angry about something and I think about that instead of schoolwork."

"Do you want to say specifically what it is, Jimmy? Maybe if you told your parents now, you'd find it easier to talk with them at home."

"If I say, Dad'll skin me."

"Now, Son, that's not true. I'm paying a lot of money to these people because I want them to help you. We've been going along with your psychiatrist, too, Dr. . . . What's his name?"

"Your father really wants to know, Jimmy. I don't believe he'll skin you no matter what you say."

"Gulp! Well, OK. I'll give you an example. Last Sunday after I mowed the lawn, I was fooling around in the house, fixing myself a Coke and a little snack in the kitchen when my father walks in. He doesn't say anything except, 'Jimmy, get that wastebasket out of the way! Empty it in the trash barrel!' And out he goes. Then he keeps after me all day. I got so mad I couldn't think of anything else in school the next day."

"Did you empty the basket?"

"No, he didn't. I did," replies Mr. Stevens angrily.

"Well, anyway, Jimmy pretty much wasted the school day. He got here in a terrible mood, and he couldn't do any studying until we got him to talk about what happened."

"He was full of resentment against us, wasn't he, Bob? Yet we weren't involved in any way. We spent most of the day working with him on his feelings."

"For God's sake. There was the trash basket sitting in the middle of the kitchen. You had to go out of your way to keep from running into it. Full to the gills! I told Jimmy to get it out of the way—to dump it. He just looked at me and didn't do a thing. I got pretty sore about it. He's an able-bodied boy, but I had to take it out myself. Why shouldn't he carry out any basket I tell him to?"

"Just like I'm some little slave or something! You never think about my side of it!"

"Your side!"

"See how sore he's getting now? How can I tell him what I feel?"

"You can try, Jimmy. Your father has feelings, too—a lot like yours, probably. He has a right to them, just as you have a right to yours."

"Why didn't you move that basket, Son?"

"I was going to before you said anything. And then when you ordered me to pick it up—you didn't ask me—you just told me—I got so angry I'd never have moved it."

Torn by conflicting impulses, Mr. Stevens is silent. At last he turns to us and laughs sheepishly, "I do get to treating my family as if they were employees in my factory. I'm used to being obeyed and no questions asked, in the plant. Things would never get done there if I didn't get right in and tell them."

"So that's it! He thinks he can run us like the workers at the plant!" Mrs. Stevens gazes at her husband in astonishment.

"How else can a man run his family?" retorts Mr. Stevens, but he blushes in spite of himself.

Mrs. Stevens is now almost in tears, but she murmurs, "It's really so, isn't it? But I could never put it in words before—even to myself. I bottle up my feelings too much—and Jimmy takes after me in that way—at least about his father's ways at home."

"Exactly. Jimmy wanted to tell you about the fact that he had intended to take out the basket on his own, but then your way of ordering him to do it enraged him. To top it all off he couldn't bring himself to talk to you about it when he knew that was what he should do. And that's what got him so upset that he couldn't do schoolwork on Monday."

"We're putting a lot of pressure on Jimmy when he's in school to speak up about himself as an alternative to acting sly or destructive in order to get 'even' for the wrongs he feels. The wastebasket affair was a real challenge for him to do at home what we are working so hard for here. Had he been able to, he could have come to school ready to study."

"This brings the whole authority question out into the open, doesn't it? Jimmy hates it when any grown-up tells him what to do."

"Do you mean that he doesn't like you to order him around either?"

"That's exactly right. There you have it. Jimmy's power struggle in school comes down pretty much to that. So we hit the issue head on. We make a point of showing him that teachers really do give commands which the students have to obey. That's one of the most important parts of the teacher-student relationship."

"Then," Mr. Stevens asks, "if I get him all riled up when I tell him what to do around the house, how are you going to get anywhere with him when you tell him to study?"

"I don't imagine you'll stop giving orders in your own house, Mr. Stevens. After all, Jimmy counts on your being in charge of certain aspects of family life. But it's different in school. Our authority doesn't come from a necessary biological and legally determined dependency. It's much more limited and comes from our reputed superiority in knowledge and maturity of judgment— which the student can choose to take advantage of or not. Our authority is effective as an element in the learning process only when the student accepts it, and even then it extends only to teaching. But it takes a long time before a boy like Jimmy, who is very confused and who has a really allergic reaction to any use of authority, learns that ours is different from yours."

"Let me add that Jimmy's not really against authority as such. In fact he likes to exercise it over others. You know he says he thinks he might be a police officer—in a squad car, of course—later on."

"What do you think, Jimmy? Is there some connection between the way you feel about your father's orders and ours?"

"Well, sort of. Sometimes when Buz—I mean Mr. Heinemann —tells me to be quiet or to start studying or something, I see red because he reminds me of Dad telling me what to do."

"We are trying to convince you that giving in to our orders, following directions—or the book, for that matter—has nothing to do with humiliating submission. That's what we're working on now."

"Meanwhile, of course we are always trying to find some subject or some idea to catch his interest."

"He's told us at home that he's studying electricity in school. He said he chose it, because he wants to learn about electronics."

"Oh, Jimmy! Marilyn exclaims reproachfully. "You're caught now—on your own hook."

Jimmy looks angrily at her, but she continues. "That's a standing joke around here. Whenever Jimmy doesn't want to follow the class schedule—especially reading—he asks if he can 'read' electricity instead. We don't either of us know a thing about electricity as a subject, and we certainly don't offer to teach it. But he brought in a book he'd bought called *Electricity Made Easy* or something like that, and he said he wanted to learn it. We thought it was only an excuse to get out of class and we told him so, but he insisted that really he was interested in learning it. So we let him try. We assigned him 'easy' amounts of reading and sent him off by himself to do it. But the same thing happened there as with everything else. He couldn't keep his mind on it. When he was alone in the next room he kept listening to our discussions in class. The result was a big fiasco, as far as learning electricity went."

"Aw, Mrs. B. It was a lot better than reading about all those dead people and old-fashioned days."

"Why, Jimmy, what a faker you can be. You love the work you've started in Mr. Heinemann's ancient history. You did a special report last week on the construction of the Pyramids. He's fascinated by them."

"That's different, Mrs. B. That's interesting. And it's not all gooey like the reading. You know what bugs me about the reading class?"

"What?"

"When you start putting feeling into it when you read aloud. Jeez, I can't stand that."

"That's what brings it to life, Jimmy."

"Yeah. You two just look silly when you do it."

"Well, here we are. I think we've come a long way, and Jimmy deserves a lot of credit. By the way, here are the results of the tests we gave him the other day."

Mr. Stevens takes the tests and looks them over while I explain the notations and scores. Marilyn takes the opportunity to talk with Mrs. Stevens about Jimmy's early years. They speak of Jimmy's younger brother who gets along quite well in school.

"The tests show that Jimmy will be able to catch up quickly when he's ready to study. He can read and spell well enough even now. His biggest problem in class is writing. His compositions are childish and boring. They're all about cars, but when we try to get him to write something more in the line of his thoughts and feelings, he just bottles up. He can't write a composition that would pass any high school's college prep course."

"What about school for next year?"

"We can't really discuss that until Jimmy makes his decision."

"What grade will he be ready for?"

"I can't say. But if he made up his mind to go on with school, and if I had to recommend a grade for him right now, I'd say that he'd have to start at the beginning of the ninth grade."

"He'd be twenty-one before graduating from high school!"

"Yes. But that's not too old, is it, Jimmy?"

"No. If I decide I want to finish my schooling I won't care if I'm a little old for my grade—as long as I don't have to go back to my old high school."

"I don't think you should do that anyway."

"The main thing is to help Jimmy get over his confusion about authority and to get him to worry less about plots of various sorts —and above all to encourage him to handle his angry and frustrated feelings about school by talking about them. We want to build up his confidence in his ability to solve academic problems as well as personal ones, and I think we are making a little headway there."

"We're really very pleased with the seriousness with which Jimmy tackles all these things, and we feel that he has made better progress than we would have predicted. He's a long way from home still, but I think we'll work very well together now."

"Especially after tonight. I think he made a big step forward when he came and talked along with us as if we were all working on the same problem. He didn't try to hide from you what he does in school, and that's what we wanted you as his parents to see and understand."

"I'll admit this has been an eye-opener for me," Mr. Stevens looks crestfallen. "I guess you folks want us to huddle a little more and decide things together more. What do you say, Son?"

"I hope you will, Dad."

"Say, there's one thing I want to bring up now that we've got this out of the way. I have a statement about the purposes of the school which I'd like you to sign. I intend to submit it to the tax people as the basis for my deducting Jimmy's tuition here from my income tax."

"What's in the statement?"

"I don't have it here. I'll send it for you to look over. You know we can deduct the psychiatrist's fees as a medical expense. So if you'll say that this is a special school for the mentally disturbed or retarded and one which doctors recommend, that'd be the sort of thing I need."

"I'm sorry, Mr. Stevens. We can't sign a statement like that. Our students are neither mentally disturbed nor retarded. And certainly not Jimmy. We are a special school, and doctors do recommend students to us, but we would not sign a statement implying that any of them is sick. If you can rephrase your statement to eliminate that implication, we'll probably sign it."

Marilyn turns to Mrs. Stevens and says, "If something crops up, please call us and we'll be glad to talk with you. I like Jimmy so much."

"I'll get you for that in the morning, Mrs. B," grins Jimmy on his way out.

VII ❦ *Trusting*

"WHAT TIME ARE WE LEAVING FOR THE MUSEUM?"

"At 10 o'clock."

"Say, how were your conferences last night?" asks Amy.

"Yeah. What was it like, Tom? I see Mrs. Bernstein and Mr. Heinemann are still alive!" Matt digs.

"Lay off, Matt. He probably doesn't want to discuss it."

"Are you kidding?" asks Jimmy. "He gave us an earful on the MTA this morning. All about how you didn't get anywhere changing his father's mind. Knowing him like I do, I think him and his old man are just alike. Stubborn."

"Tom's right. We didn't get very far with his father. But that wasn't what was so depressing about it."

"No, it was Tom himself."

"Why, what'd he do?"

"I didn't do anything."

"You certainly didn't. You didn't back us up at all when we were trying to explain your problems to your parents."

"You were wrong about me."

"That's just what you kept saying."

"Did you think we were wrong about you when we said that you were much more intelligent than your records showed?"

"Well . . . uh—"

"Did you think we were wrong when we said you had a lot of fantasies running through your mind and that they kept you from concentrating on schoolwork?"

"Uh . . . uh, again."

"Well, that's the point. When we're talking here, you don't say we're wrong about everything."

We have scheduled an outside trip to the Museum of Fine Arts.

However, even when we cancel our regular classes, we still must deal with whatever is uppermost in the students' minds before carrying through our plans. The parent conferences continue over a two-week period, and still cause anxiety. Ned was particularly trying in his, and Tom's was almost a disaster.

"You tried to say that I should go to a psychiatrist. You were wrong about that. They don't do any good," Tom complains.

"That's your father's opinion, not ours. You've admitted that the kids here have benefited from theirs—so it's not your opinion either."

"My father knows."

"You're foolish. He knows a lot of things better than you do, but that doesn't mean that you can't have your own opinions—especially when you can find support for them."

"That's it, Tom. We were trying to back you up last night, but you quit. You tried to turn every one of our observations into a joke, and you even lied about some things."

"A lot of it was a joke. Besides, you can't tell me what to think."

"If you think we're no good—which was about the way you made it sound last night—why do you want to keep coming here?"

"We've paid a lot of money and I should be getting something out of it."

"But if you're not, why not admit it and go try something else?"

"The plain truth, Bob, is that Tom is in a jam. He can't agree with us if he thinks our views oppose his father's. He's too afraid."

"Do you mean he can't have his own ideas?"

"Well, I think he can't choose between his father and us."

A dangerous conflict of loyalties is not born when students participate in parent-teacher meetings, but it may be quickly exposed there. Tom has long seen adults as mutually exclusive authorities. He has long feared that following our suggestions will draw terrible paternal reprisals down upon his head. Every day at school stirs the conflict. When we probe his mind for the truth, he is hearing his father say psychological investigations are worthless. Tom feels forbidden to tell us what he is thinking; he dares not explain what makes him too angry to study. The paternal interference extends to rivalrous disagreements with our methods of teaching algebra or the use of fractions instead of decimals. Yet it is not the disagreement itself that makes the situation dangerous or even difficult; it is the father's competitive, disparaging, and deeply hostile tone that warns Tom of peril.

Of course, to all our students the conflicts leading to independence are a clash of violent, implacable, and unshaded opposites. Even if they can conceive of a "third" position, they do not see how it is to survive. Our joint conferences are not supposed to force them to choose between parents and teachers, though at first they think so. Through open discussion of differences we want to prepare a platform of opinions and judgments which the student can incorporate into a point of view of his own, no matter what side the adults take.

"If Tom can't stand it, it'll be a waste of real talent," Matt speaks with vigor.

"Tom's very intelligent, and he ought to stay here and work things out for himself."

"What did you think of *my* parents, Mrs. Bernstein?" Ned asks.

"They're awfully smart. You come by your brains honestly."

"Yeah, they're smart, all right. But not about me."

"How can you expect them to be? You try so hard to fool them."

"I got the impression that your parents have not yet understood the school very well. And I think that you don't help them to, either."

"It wouldn't do to get you all together very much. And my mother doesn't understand with her head. She just feels things. But why did you tell them I wouldn't help you move the furniture in the school when you were fixing the rug? That was a dirty trick."

"You showed there the present state of your selfishness. It's the kind of problem they have with you, too."

"When you tell them things like that, it just makes things more uncomfortable for me at home. Don't you know that? You can see why I hesitate to trust you."

"Well, we didn't bring up the book-stealing episode. Isn't that what you were most afraid of?"

"Oh! You wouldn't dare to do that to me!"

"What do you know? You're counting on us not to betray you after all. That's news."

"Of course. Though that rug business certainly was a betrayal."

"Actually, if you want to know, I think you betrayed us, and almost disastrously."

"How?"

"You did the same thing Tom did. Whenever we tried to show your parents how you really are, you'd disagree with us—or refuse to corroborate what we said."

"Well, do you expect me to go along with you and accuse myself?"

"Come off it, Ned. After all this time you know we aren't accusing you. We're trying to understand as much as we can about you."

"I know it today, but last night it felt different. When you were all lined up there it looked as though everybody was set to gun me down. Don't say it! I know. I know. I'm wrong."

"If you couldn't admit that today—and if you hadn't come through with the truth at last, I'd be ready to quit."

That meeting started badly. Ned's parents were ashamed to have him come to RSS, and Ned, hoping to keep us all in separate compartments, had done nothing to help his parents understand our work. There seemed to be no common ground. We kept trying to get Ned to talk to his parents as candidly as he talks to us in school, but whatever characteristic or incident we described, Ned contradicted.

"What was the revelation?" asks Amy.

"Wait. We were getting nowhere fast. Then Ned's father began to complain about the school's name. He wanted us to call it Fresh Pond Hall."

"I favor Mrs. Bernstein's name for it: Catskin Academy."

"What's so funny about that?" asks Ned.

"Because we're going to give you catskins instead of sheepskins when you graduate from these ivy halls."

"Is that what the mold on the wall is?"

"C'mon. C'mon. Get to the point."

"OK, Jimmy. OK. Ned's father thinks a name like REMEDIAL SCHOLASTIC SERVICES will look bad on his son's record years from now when he goes to be employed."

The father's excessive concern for appearances had shaken up

Ned. These meetings are anything but manipulated happenings. They are a kind of crucible in which deep feelings may boil up in all the participants; the truth will out. In this case Ned began to show his angry feelings for the first time in the meeting. Soon he explained his secret wars against teachers; his mounting fury made his parents speechless. With tears in his eyes he talked about his teachers "slashing" at him, and he described his "slashing" vengeance. Vividly he recalled his fifth grade where, he said, the trouble began. It was when the teacher had been explaining something to the class while he, Ned, was talking to a neighbor. The teacher stopped, and sarcastically asked Ned to give her permission to teach the class. Although he felt attacked by her tone, he misunderstood her meaning and thought she really was asking his permission to speak. His intense egotism collided with the truth, turning all his later school experience into a personal vendetta. He "knew" that teachers were out to get him, that learning was their trap. Ned's interpretation of that small incident came out at the meeting, shocking his parents and surprising us.

"You know, Ned's family is used to supportive tutoring, a perpetual hand-holding and back-patting combined with much talk about 'poor word-attack.' It was quite a blow for them to feel the depth of his emotions."

"I'll bet they thought you were cruel and abusive to their darling Neddy! I know that's what my parents thought," Franny says.

"Did they, Ned?"

"Well, I wasn't supposed to say."

"Don't then. But Franny, in your parents' case, they said what they thought. What we are after surprised them as much as it does Ned's folks, but they want to know more about it and struggle to understand a viewpoint completely new to them. Ned's parents are much more defensive, I think."

"My parents think you're too rough, too," Alden offers, "but they say sometimes you have to be. They get pretty sore at you, but they seem to like the fact that you puncture some of my empty dreams and bring me back to the facts, man. Facts."

However embarrassing it is to drop pretenses, reaffirmation of reality reassures student and parent alike. When the student allows parents and teachers to combine their separate bits of information about him, the turmoils of adolescence become subject to rational treatment. Gone is some of the fear of punishment should his parents discover the depths to which he can sink; going is the greater fear that a unified and consistent knowledge of his character would, in parental hands, become a powerful weapon against him.

"Well, Ned, so much for that," Marilyn's eye is determined. "We'll have to see how it goes. Let's start with settling the stolen book matter."

"Why?"

"Oh, Mrs. B, let's get going. We want to go to the Museum."

"Yes, Marilyn. I don't think we have time for it."

"Just a few minutes, I want to settle this issue today. We can't let it go unresolved."

"I just hope he won't get all 'psyched up' like Tom," Matt says. "Don't forget we'll all be seen with him at the Museum."

"It's not so serious, Mrs. B," Ned offers. "And anyway, there isn't much to settle."

"Yes, there is. You have to return the book."

"I don't see why."

"That's probably not true. But if it is true, all the more reason to have it out now."

"What do you mean?"

"If your conscience is defective, if you don't want to do what is right and avoid what is wrong, we can't teach you anyway."

"Why not? My principle is that I'll do whatever is good for *me*. If it's going to be good for me to learn and do well in school, I'll reform."

"Oh, so you think that all you have to do is come to a decision and then you'll act?"

"Yes, I do."

"Well, Ned, you are wrong about that. You have—as I've told you before—a very exaggerated idea of your ability to control yourself. For instance, when I tell you to do a certain assignment in algebra you get angry at me and turn yourself off. How are you going to stop doing that—unless you do get over getting angry at me?"

"Uh, well . . . maybe."

"Or take your usual reaction to teachers. It's our job to see that you learn. According to you the responsibility is all ours. You happen to know that's cockeyed. Right?"

"Right. I'll admit it now for the sake of argument."

"OK. Every time we have a class your first reaction is the same as it's always been. You only begin to learn by yourself after we have an argument and I make the point again."

"Are you trying to tell me now—after all this time—that I can't change, Mrs. B? Boy, that's . . ."

"No, Ned, I'm not. I'm only trying to say that you probably won't make sudden, miraculous changes in patterns that you've clung to and even elaborated for years. You can't discard them without solving some of your problems. When you make up your mind to do well in school you are only at the beginning of an involved and difficult process."

"I guess you're getting back to the book."

"Yes, and your conscience."

"What's the connection?"

"You take great pride in your total selfishness, but I think you rely upon it only because a long time ago you were so bitterly disappointed, that you stopped trusting everyone. Your egotism is a retreat, not an advance! Trust is indispensable in the solution of learning problems. A student who always takes and never gives cannot use our help in overcoming his own weaknesses."

"And?"

"Organized school learning requires students to give. You have to give attention, give various proofs of achievement, and give the teacher the right to tell you what to do. You may even give trust and respect for the teacher's competence and more experienced judgment."

"You don't want much, do you?"

"Yes, it's a lot, but there's more. You took that book because you wanted it and reasoned falsely that you were not hurting anyone. Basically you took it because you felt it your right to take. You could easily pay the two dollars the book cost, but egotism prevents you. When you return the book or the money it will be a sign that you are willing to give—at least to give back—even when you don't feel like it. Returning it may make it easier for you to see that you can't estimate the damage you did the real owner and that you were really wrong to steal. If you return the book today I will know you can trust us enough to accept our judgment no matter how much resistance you feel. In a nutshell, if you can't give *us* a reassurance about yourself now, when we need it and demand it, I for one see no hope in our continuing to offer you help."

"Mrs. B, you zeroed in on that one, but you can be just as long-winded as Mr. H. When do we leave?" Jimmy breaks in.

"I agree with what Mrs. B has said," I add. "Since we are going to pass the bookstore on our way to the Museum, I'd be glad to have you ride with me. I'll wait outside while you run in. If you brought the book in here today you can just put it back on the shelf—or you can pay the money to the clerk. You won't have to say who you are. Just say that you took a book without paying for it, and that you've realized it and want to pay now."

"You mean you want action today?"

"Yes."

"You don't care about my telling my name or apologizing and all that?"

"No."

"And what if I say no? I mean I'm broke and I don't have the money, and maybe I just want to keep the book."

"I think we've been pretty clear. We'll have to stop working with you."

"You certainly put on the pressure, man!"

"Why do you feel pressure, Ned?" asks Amy. "You're always saying that they're wrong about you and don't really understand. If that's so you won't lose anything by ending it."

"Oh shut up, Amy."

"I'm surprised at all of you," says Marilyn. "You jump on one another like sharks. I know you have sympathy for each other about some of these things. Why don't you show it now, when it counts?"

"It's always the same, Marilyn. They can't stand to have us give too much attention to anyone else."

"We are putting on the pressure, Ned, because we want you to stay."

"You're threatening."

"Oh, don't imitate Tom. You know better than that. Mrs. B has fully explained the case. If we quit with you we'll just be acknowledging the truth—that you cannot respond to us."

"Is there a deadline today?"

"No. But soon. Today seems like a good time to settle it."

"It takes a lot of thought. And I've been giving it some, but I want to think more about the choices you're giving me now. I'll let you know when we come back from the Museum."

"Good. All right. I guess we're about ready to go."

This museum trip is a welcome change, a chance to do something light and different. Although it has academic interest to the history class members, it is a new or unfamiliar cultural experience to all. They are excited, but, once inside, they radiate a natural dignity and harmony altogether unexpected from any observation of their daily RSS behavior. However, when we take them to lunch, their unity gives way. They are delighted to have us "treat" in the sense of taking them out to eat, but they attach an extraordinary importance to it. It is as if our giving and their taking food might be a symbolic reference to a long ago child-adult exchange that was never completed. This early failure at home plays a role in their later learning disabilities and explains their taking our "treat" as a transaction ultimately akin to our giving and their taking knowledge. Thus their newfound dignity and harmony are threatened by events at the table, and the students who trust us least are the most vulnerable. Tom, for example, eats, but rejects the meal as in any sense a reciprocal transaction. He is unpledged and demonstrates it by stealing a knife and fork as "souvenirs." Matt and Jimmy try vainly to dissuade him from this disruptive act, finally turning to us for help. Their stand, as much as Tom's, indicates the complex interconnections of giving and taking, teaching and learning.

Ned rides back to school with me. He is quiet and thoughtful while the rest are laughing at my slowpoke driving. The incident with Tom is full of meaning for him, and it is obvious that we are at a favorable moment for bringing the book episode to a close.

"Shall I go by the bookstore on the way back, Ned? I can do it easily and we'll wait while you dash in with the money."

"Don't rush me. I'm thinking."

"OK. I just hate to lose an opportunity."

"Yeah."

But he says no more and soon we are back at school. Ned's mood continues, and Marilyn, also seeing in him a readiness, speaks once again with insistent directness.

"I think you're deciding what to do right now, Ned. So let's get it over."

"And if I don't?"

"Oh cut it out. You know."

"I won't pay for it. I can't afford the money. I only have $16 and that has to last until May."

"You can easily get the money. But you don't have to pay for it. If you had it here we could wrap it up and mail it back right now."

"What makes you think I don't have it here?"

"You always talk as though it were under your mattress or something."

"Did I ever say it wasn't here?"

"No. But don't be silly. Is it here?"

"You're sure I can mail it and I don't have to take it in myself?"

"Yes."

"Well, it's here. Want to see it?"

"I do. The Mona Lisa could hardly be more valuable judging from all the importance this affair gets around here."

"OK. Here. Man, who would have thought I'd give in like this?"

"I've got some wrapping paper. Look, I'll even wrap it for you. Thank goodness, Ned. I'm so glad about this."

"You ought to be."

"What are you doing?"

"Writing a note to go with the book. So the guy'll know why he's getting it in the mail."

"You don't have to go into detail, Ned."

"If I do it at all I'm going to explain what it is."

"Look, Marilyn. He's even signing his name!"

"Ned, you don't have to. All we insist upon is sending it back."

"I know that. I know I don't have to sign my name. But, after all, why be so childish? What's in a name?"

Ned's selfishness is now dented. He "gives in," as he must if we are to teach him; the obligation he accepts sets a certain tone in the student-teacher relationship which for him determines its intrinsic development and meaning. With this our active interest in the issue ceases. The specific ethical stamp of a student's conscience belongs more to his parents and other societal forces.

VIII ❧ *Parents and Therapists*

ALTHOUGH WE COUNTED almost exclusively upon our relationships with the students, we were constantly aware of the other influences which shaped so significantly, if indirectly, the course of all we tried to do. Of these, the parents and the psychotherapists were our direct concern. Because we set our sights for complete frankness and cooperation without having enough time and wisdom to achieve such goals fully, we often felt that we did not deal with either group as ably as we should have. Generally the psychiatrists told us that we were mistaken in our direct efforts to explain the students' problems to parents or to induce in them a change of attitude that seemed desirable to us. The therapists believed that willy-nilly we had made a primary alliance with the students that somehow excluded candid discussions with their parents. They recommended the employment of a social worker, to mediate between parents and teachers. Only one psychiatrist said it was important for parents to hear directly from us, so that they might understand our position that when the student made a choice, we held him significantly responsible for the educational consequences.

Our own view was that whatever alliances we made in favor of the students, we were making none against the parents; indeed, we had to believe, even when there were unconscious negative impulses at work, that the parents also wanted to promote their children's welfare. We had a firm conviction that school problems involve parents, teachers, and students both intellectually and passionately, and that it would not do for a cool third person to hold us at bay.

None of the parents ever suggested alternatives for our dealing directly with psychiatrists although they often complained about their own inability to get information from the doctors who treated their children.

The parents' ambitions, attitudes, and feelings about education often precipitated or aggravated the learning problems. Though we were sure that the students must assume the major responsibility for solving their own problems, it was obvious that the influence of their parents might seriously interfere. At the outset we knew we ought to try to help parents modify their attitudes and make a positive contribution toward our common goal of academic success. The trouble was that much destructive influence came from unstated and usually unconscious factors which the parents would have been shocked or ashamed to recognize. Close work with parents even if feasible would have aroused hostile suspicions in the children, and we would stand to lose on this score. We were teachers, not therapists or social workers. Our sympathies were with the children. Where there was conflict between parents and children—as there usually was—we supported the.youngsters, though not necessarily "against" their parents. Still we did tend to blame parents for making our work harder, for their lack of sympathy, or their obduracy. As teachers it was our job to report our findings to them and discuss the ideas we worked with in school, stating simply the conditions we required. When we found out what the reasons for school failure were, we hoped to share the knowledge with them no matter how remote their way of thinking. Ideally, with their collaboration we would bear down on the problems and work out the answers in harmonious accord.

We knew about the powerfully ambivalent wishes of parents who had to resort to professionals for help with their children. Some parents communicate their own troubles by means of the children's shortcomings, and no matter what is said, a solution of the child's school problem is the last thing they would want. Our seemingly simple recommendations might disturb the pattern of family relationships and therefore become emotionally inadmissible whatever the rational content. But as teachers we had to expect that these parents could handle their own hurt and anger when their long-held values were challenged, hoping they could transcend immediate tensions and frustrations and allow reason to reign. We foresaw great upheavals—and even encouraged them.

If parents suddenly realized their part in school problems, the suffering induced by such insights could propel them toward new ideas and changed behavior.

Parents were uncertain about the boundaries in their relationships with us. Those who supposed we would blame them sometimes made confessions whose irrelevance embarrassed us. If telling us relieved their tensions, it did not solve school problems. One man told us that his son's school problems might have been caused by his poor performance in bed with his wife.

In recent discussions with a number of parents whose children had spent a year or more at RSS, most thought we had helped, though some reserved judgment. They tried to recall their first thoughts and feelings to trace the changes they experienced.

Defeated and resentful, they had brought their children to RSS for the first interviews. Their feelings of hopelessness did not mean that they really offered to turn over their children to us nor did their perplexity open them to new ideas. They were critical of everything they saw in the school, and in expressing their reservations they reasserted their underlying determination to postpone that "evil day" when facts had to be faced. They showed their reluctance to "turn over" to us any part of the management of their children. One parent, who later said that her child "could lead people into trouble with both hands tied behind her back," admitted that she first looked askance at RSS because she thought the other children might have a bad influence on her daughter. A mother told us she envisioned her daughter's being "dragged down by such weak associates." Parents might admit something was wrong with their own children, but they "knew" that their classmates should be children without such problems!

Although in our interviews we conscientiously explained and actually demonstrated what we would do with the students, almost all the parents reported being puzzled. It was probably with our first written report and the meeting which followed it that the parents began to form an accurate picture of RSS. We worked with a student for nearly eight weeks before the first report was sent. Reports were usually long and represented our best efforts both to formulate our ideas about the child and to express them simply and plainly. For most parents, the reports were of great importance since they could and often did study them. "Your reports were part of your philosophy," they told us, "honest and direct. We were relieved that you knew our child so well." "Your reports were brilliant but we had to get a dictionary and go over and over it until we really understood those letters . . . I'm keeping all the reports you sent us. If anyone ever asks us what kind of child he is, I'll just hand them over."

This later enthusiasm did not exist when the time came for the meetings to discuss the reports. The parents were eager to talk to us, but they were loath to do so in the presence of the child. For them, it was customary to deal with school authorities in private, but they got used to discussing openly sensitive questions, though some of them still resented our insistence. One parent said, "You had a fetish against privacy," and there were others who felt as he did. "Suitable for research, perhaps, but not therapeutic in the least. . . . Just a little honest sneakiness would have helped."

Most parents disliked the policy, but they eventually did welcome a dogged pursuit of openness. "I fought you all along about my daughter's knowing everything we talked about, but I have to admit that she benefited greatly because you kept on insisting . . . Your round table meetings exasperated me. You were so rough I would rather have sent a substitute, but after all the difficulty was only half my son's. The other half was ours."

One purpose of the meetings was to inform the parents, but another was to provide the means by which a student might have mature and honest exchanges with his parents. This meant that the student could agree with his parents for his own reasons and disagree with them as well, without fear of annihilation. It also meant that he would have to understand his parents better. It was a revelation to some to see parents reaching an insight all had been groping for, and students were amazed when tears of recognition rather than reproach stood in their parents' eyes. They were equally astounded to hear us speak openly and critically in front of parents as we did normally in school. We frequently argued and disagreed with parents, to prove that verbal combat between adults and adolescents was not only possible but necessary to maintain close relationships. We sometimes took the side of the student and defended him vigorously against the point of view his parents were taking. The students were gratified to have our support, but what we wanted them to learn was that though they might not always win, they could and should argue. The parents did not always approve of our alignment with their child, as they saw it, against them. One father expressed what most seemed to feel, "I thought, 'maybe they're downgrading me, making him change his picture of me, treating me as excess baggage of his life, and putting me out of the picture!'" Another parent admitted rather sheepishly, "You can't have neutrality if you are going to know both our daughter *and* us."

Neutrality, of course, was not our goal. Yet, we wanted to show that the deceptions to which students resorted, and their serious weaknesses, could be treated as problems to be solved by rational analysis and action. At the meetings we could be as critical of the student in front of his parents as we had been in school. One parent commented, "I was glad, for once, to have a chance not to be the ogre." Others conceded that there was value in our candor, but regretted it as a two-edged sword. "My son had a structure around him that had to be knocked down and knocked down brutally. You did it, but no part should have been done in front of us . . . You seemed to be in combat with him, and your harshness with my child made me uncomfortable and resentful. I wanted to defend him, but feared that I might betray some greater purpose of what you were trying to achieve. You made me choose between him and you." One mother took us to task for finding fault with her son although she agreed with our criticism. "This helped us," she said, "but did it help him?" We were surprised at the vehemence with which some parents expressed their shock at our open objections to their children's behavior. "You bore down on him more heavily than necessary; you left him bleeding . . . You badgered, you dissected him, you pushed too much and too hard. Couldn't you have tempered it with a few little white lies?"

A few parents believed that victory over learning problems demanded an end to illusions and self-deceptions. "I admired your obstinate attachment to bare reality . . . Many people can't speak home truths or hear them. We were glad you could. All this had to be . . . We feared that such an unsure child would be damaged by the whole truth. Now we see that instead she was helped.

. . . She was dying to escape into fantasy and she might never have gotten back to the real world if you hadn't been there pounding . . . There was no fantasy about the mess they were in. It was reality at RSS."

It had taken some of these parents a long time to reach these conclusions. They began to know us and understand the seriousness of the issues at the middle of the first year, after two reports and at least two conferences. While we struggled with the parents over the issue of homework, some of them were taking a more positive attitude toward the whole group. "At RSS for the first time, my son could say to himself, I am not alone . . . The students saw that their troubles didn't make them freaks . . . It was helpful to see other kids struggle with the same feelings . . . I noticed how each student knew the problems of the others . . . Sometimes another student knew better than you what was wrong. He could get in there and help you help." A few, whose children were in psychiatric treatment, took the occasion to express criticism of the therapists on the grounds that they remained too distant from the larger arena of the student's operations. "You saw through her at last, but my daughter hoodwinked the first psychiatrist we took her to. An intelligent child can do that sometimes if the doctor listens only to her . . . Psychiatry is the last gasp. People like you can do much more with understanding and sensitivity, by working directly on the problem as it is lived out and fulminates . . . This may be heresy, but my son is better without psychiatry. You folks help him more." Of course we understood that they were alienated from psychiatry because they thought it had failed them. We agreed that our work might be more appropriate for the solution of learning problems in certain specific cases, but we tried to point out that neither was the substitute for the other. Indeed, we relied upon psychotherapy to deal with those preoccupations that had no place in school.

While parents were digesting the psychological aspects of our work and adjusting to the radical departure of our joint conferences, they still pressed for evidence of school achievement. For a long time we viewed the standardized testing program as one way to meet this anxiety. The parents naturally worried about the academic level at which their children were working, and they hoped it would rise at least high enough to make regular school placement possible. The parents' point of view was well expressed by one father who said, "Well, you are the only school I know of that doesn't force learning, and that's good. A kid needs a chance to think things over, but I'm mighty disappointed that the points aren't piling up while he's making up his mind." At least one mother recognized, though, that her son was working at something. "He always came back from RSS," she said, "looking as if he had been working in a mine and was exhausted. His psychiatrist sent him home happy and calm."

One of the most difficult ideas for parents to accept was the element of choice about completing school. They considered it axiomatic that school was the only road and could hardly imagine that their children might develop into mature, successful adults without ever fitting into the educational lock step. Yet there was a possibility—sometimes a probability—that a particular child could not make a personal commitment to academic learning. His I.Q. might be high, but his academic motivation overpowered by other drives and ambitions. If a student chose not to develop through academic learning, or if he had to put it off for an indefinite time, we hoped his parents could accept the decision. But when we told them, "This child should not be going to school—at least not now," they misunderstood. They thought we were labeling their children unintelligent. No matter how desperately the child needed to leave school, some parents could not sanction it even temporarily. They complained of being "hit over the head" when we advised them to allow their children to leave high school or college and look elsewhere for answers. When we were pleading with them to look the obvious right in the eye, we were accused of discouraging the young. They told us, "To allow and even try to call forth such negativism is like cutting out all the foundations. You can't do it. The positive approach would have worked. You can never understand what telling us our daughter should quit school meant to us."

A number of parents remained untouched by what happened at RSS, and became hostile to the point where the conflict between school and home was too great for the student to bear. We parted company in such cases.

Others were dissatisfied with the results of our work and some blamed us for the failures. One mother thought we asked far too much of her thirteen-year-old son when we expected him to assume a share of responsibility for deciding his future in school. Most recognized the complexity of their children's problems. "In all honesty we don't blame RSS. This was an unusually formidable and perhaps hopeless problem, from an academic viewpoint. You properly sized him up as not having any real or lasting motivation, and he still has not . . . You certainly tided him over in the acute period which must have been almost backbreaking for you. I think you gave him a lot of security and love of reading which has never left him. . . . It took RSS to discover that my daughter always needed the physical presence of the teacher to lean against, and she leaned hard. Her dependence was too deep to get over, too enormous to put aside. You couldn't help her there, but you did bring her to see that unless she was working with the teacher, she was just not comfortable in school."

The parents of more successful students gave our approach a wide range of credits. "Better understanding of the student was given to the parent, and thereby the student was definitely helped" . . . "My daughter benefited more from our change in attitude towards her than from what she got directly at school. You showed *us* the way to help her" . . . "If you had just kept my son from becoming a juvenile delinquent that would have been enough, but you did more. You turned him into a professional student" . . . "This was the turning point in my daughter's life. Suddenly she became a whole person" . . . "You restored in my son an ethical approach to life. He went back to high school and graduated, a different boy." . . . "You helped us tremendously by pointing out that if we would relax and stop forcing her, she would be only too glad to look to us for guidance and our opinions. It was the pushing she couldn't take. When we learned to talk *with* her instead of *at* her, she even began to be openly affectionate." They told us too that RSS had helped in the area of student-teacher relationships. "He learned that all teachers weren't SOB's. He'd lost faith and you made it possible for him to respect the good ones and live with the bad ones" . . . "Instead of flying off in a rage and withdrawing either mentally or physically, he now goes to the teacher and says, 'I have to talk with you!' " . . . "When he said, 'That teacher is a bastard, but I am still going to learn what she is teaching!' I thought I'd pass out."

We were not satisfied that we did everything possible to help parents understand. We knew what we did was wrong for some, but it was consistent with our ideas at RSS and essential to our integrity. Face-saving tact, lofty detachment, "scientific" suspension of judgment were not for teachers at RSS. We taught our students the value of personal struggle and commitment and took the brickbats along with the bouquets. Now we wonder how many parents share the feelings of one who said, "You ought to be sent into the public schools with your ideas and try to apply them preventively. It would take a couple of decades before they'd accept you. I can see you both now, whizzing down the long corridors in your wheelchairs!"

If the parents were a problem for us to deal with, at least we began our relationship with the advantage of having conferred with them at the school. We were able to establish a pattern for keeping in contact with one another principally through the planned reports and meetings, and we had been able to size each other up as personalities.

With the psychotherapists the situation was not ordered in advance and a student could begin at the school without his therapist having any specific knowledge of our school, without any direct contact between therapist and teachers, without any agreement about whether or not we would deal with each other and if we did how it would be done.

We were ill-informed about the therapists, not knowing, for example, to what school of psychiatry the individual belonged or what his attitude was toward the alliances often made among the three sets of adult powers—parents, therapists, and teachers. Without a clear understanding of these alliances we never knew what backing a student had.

With little communication and mutual planning from which to proceed, our exchanges, or lack of them, were casual, even haphazard. The great ambiguity of the situation allowed everyone to assume what he would, and so the gap which traditionally divides teachers and psychiatrists was at RSS scarcely bridged and possibly widened.

The matter of communication is becoming a more significant problem because more students in all sorts of schools are entering therapy. Even in RSS there was a marked change over the years. At first about one fourth of the group were in therapy. The proportion was five sixths in our last year and the kinds of students were just about the same. Few students received intensive treatment or saw their therapists more than once a week. However, we relied upon the doctors as important and powerful allies, recognizing how crucial it was for us to be working in some sort of accord. An uneasy relationship was inevitably reflected in the child we both sought to help. Impressed by their scientific training and knowledge of what often seemed to us uncharted seas, we did not think to ask for the reciprocity essential to formal relations defining the terms under which each of us would be working. From the perspective of time it seems painfully obvious that we should have tried to work out at the very start, with each psychotherapist, a definite plan for communication or at the least an agreement about the absence of it. Working individually with varying theories about the treatment of learning problems and the personalities of particular doctors as well as our own, we might have avoided some of the problems which arose from assumptions and expectations about therapists which remained untested and virtually unchanged because of the separation. Instead, we were plagued with problems in our dealings with them and often felt disappointed, sometimes frustrated and angry.

We assumed that the doctors referring students to us or sending their own patients to us would want to know who we were and something about our school. We thought they would want to speak with us at some length about our approach or even visit classes in action. None of the doctors did this, and we concluded that they were not interested. Now we know that this is the general pattern. In the realm of "special" schools the choices are few if they exist at all and the attitude of most doctors seems to be that "good" people can be relied upon to be conducting "good" schools. The tremendously over-scheduled time of "good" psychiatrists does not permit them the kind of exploration we envisioned and that they ideally respect. Several of them told us later that even had they the time to evaluate schools they would not feel qualified to judge them since they had not been trained in education. Although they conceded that they could probably pick out bad schools the ability to prescribe good ones was more elusive. When we approached them for information in writing this book they told us they could seldom guide us when we were at sea, for they did not know how to teach these children. In the absence of scientific answers to learning problems therapists were content to let us be the "experts." One doctor told a parent, "I don't really know what it is they do out there, but I do know it works."

We assumed that the doctors would be utterly honest with us about their patients. We thought it would be just as dangerous for them as for us to have the student in a situation which developed considerable pressures when he could not withstand such pressures. Some of the doctors soft-pedaled the disturbance of their patients in order to get us to accept them and in these instances the placement usually failed to work out, even for a year. Now we can see that certain doctors were afraid to tell us very much about their patients because they thought the information would alarm us and would not contribute to our teaching. The doctors had no way of knowing how we would handle psychiatric information. We expected to be treated as collaborators in the healing of troubled children and thought we could handle the truth about our students. The doctors had no way of measuring us in this regard.

We assumed that we were partners with the doctors in working very hard at central issues with the students. Every day we seriously approached their refusals and we believed that the therapists acknowledged our part as important if separate from theirs. We did not account for the variety of attitudes which psychiatrists could have about the role of school and teachers in the solution of learning problems. For doctors who saw their patient's schooling as part of life experience which essentially should continue undisturbed during the course of his therapy, a school like ours would be merely a source of mischief. To such psychiatrists any intervention in the environment of the child distorts the nature of therapy and becomes manipulation with very negative and contaminating connotations. For them school should be a holding operation in a world which should stand as still as possible while they work on the child's problems in a stable environment. When basic emotional conflicts are resolved in the child's unconscious, the school problems will resolve themselves, too. It is said that the unconscious knows no time, but children are growing and developing during their therapy and if they fall behind academically the result may be serious dislocations of a different kind from those with which they started emotionally. For doctors who wanted as little outside change as possible the basic principles of RSS must have been anathema. Straight baby-sitting would have been far more acceptable.

Others, more willing to assign the teacher a real part in the solution of learning problems, conceive that part as mechanical and secondary. The Judge Baker Guidance Center in Boston has been studying learning problems intensively for more than ten years and has concluded among many other things that the tutor is an integral part of their resolution. They found that tutors uncover specific school material not revealed in psychotherapy but useful to the therapists. When doctors tried to become teachers themselves to get at this information they undermined their position as therapists. So they asked the tutors to gather information for them to use later in psychotherapy. The teachers in that arrangement did not have the responsibility or the satisfaction of using the "gold" they panned. Separate areas of work were clearly demarcated so that each knew exactly what the other would do. None of the psychiatrists with whom we worked ever asked us to operate with them in this way, but it was another attitude toward teachers which militated against the conception of truly colleagual relationships as we sought them.

Even the doctors who granted us a full-blown place for our work did not wish to try to work things out together during the process of the child's education at our school. The so-called team approach in which members of various disciplines do work together and confer regularly about the progress of children they are trying to help seemed not to apply to us. When doctors failed to acknowledge or respond to the long reports we sent about students we felt put off.

Yet when we discussed these reports with them later several doctors remarked on their excellence. How grateful we would have been to know of this appreciation in the midst of our struggles with their patients. Their silence puzzled and depressed us. Instead of interpreting it as they said they meant it, "Things are going well there so best let it continue undisturbed," we often thought they didn't have enough regard for our whole operation to bother commenting about what we were doing.

We always assumed that we were teachers, not therapists of any kind. It now seems very clear that the doctors often considered us therapists of a sort and it is easy to see why. At RSS our first approaches to the student were parallel to those used by a therapist. We began by making an alliance with the student, asking him how he saw his problems and what his reactions were. We asked why he behaved as he did and we required him to examine his present unsatisfactory adjustment. Like the doctors, we withstood intensely angry feelings as part of the process of getting to know the individual. Indeed, one psychologist said, "Now I understand what you are doing here, Sector Therapy. You limit yourselves to school dynamics."

We were teachers, not therapists. Dr. Felix Deutsch defined psychotherapy as "any considered and competent medical endeavor directed for the improvement of the individual, based upon the understanding of the psychodynamics involved and the needs of the individual under treatment." Our prime object was intellectual development through pedagogical not medical endeavors.

Doctors repeatedly probe the conflict of wishes within the students, to resolve them. Their goal is the student's general maturation. We examined the conflict to discover and support the side leading to academic success. The doctor's work with his patient lasts as long as they both agree it is helpful. Our time limits with students were subject to pressure from the graded educational system. The therapist seeks anonymity and avoids judgments in order to unearth subjective feelings. Starting with the factual details, he works toward general modes of feeling. We exploited our personalities to guide students away from subjective states, toward an interest in academic matters. In therapy, a verbalization of feelings develops emotional issues further. We sought statements of feelings to release energy and harness it for learning. Therapists regard events of school life as symbolic and symptomatic of nuclear disorders extending backward to the student's beginnings. For us, these same school events were the reality with which we dealt.

Many therapists say that learning difficulties are stubborn to deal with and claim that even when other troubled areas clear up in the course of treatment, learning blocks often remain. They agree that the answer is frequently to be found in the classroom itself. As one psychologist observed, "Often one cannot get over the learning problem directly through psychiatry. Direct work on the teaching situation is needed. The teacher is in the only sure position to get the specific, concrete reactions of the child facing each step of the learning process as it occurs in school." Many of the doctors considered RSS a center where disaffection with learning was openly dealt with.

Differences in our point of view and function led us to demand far more from the student in terms of current performance than did his therapist. We invariably treated the student as a stronger person than did the therapist who sometimes censured us for asking too much. Sometimes the students seemed to echo their therapists when we held them to responsibilities; they would protest that their problems stemmed from the unconscious and were beyond deliberate control; or they would report working on emotional problems in therapy, intending to postpone the solution of school problems until therapy had succeeded. Time and again they wanted to buck our rule against doctors' appointments that would cut into school time. They shifted gears when they shuttled between school and therapy. As patients they looked into the past, seeking freedom from neurosis at the point of origin. As students at RSS they were pressed to look forward, albeit with backward glances. We urged the student to scramble over impediments which he could not move.

The irony was that this very clear distinction between school and therapy which apparently was helpful to the student got us into another problem in dealing with the psychiatrists. Because they viewed the student's behavior from the standpoint of pathology they were hardly alarmed and disturbed when the students "got worse" or acted quite sick. Judging our students by conventional social standards we became concerned about safety when crises arose and would anxiously telephone the doctor. Generally hard to reach, with complicated schedules necessitating many calls and several days of message-leaving before contact was made, the doctors seemed to elude us when we felt we needed them most. Sitting and waiting where we could always be reached our feelings of urgency would become heightened and when the doctor finally called we would recount the situation which concerned us with great relief at having heard from him. How dashed we were when the response was usually one of cool acceptance and apparent lack of concern about our emergency. Was he being evasive? Didn't he realize how serious this was? We did not see that from his framework of pathology he did not interpret the behavior in the same way that we did nor was he very worried about it. Trained to accept the idea that much of human behavior is determined by non-logical, irrational forces he tried to take a detached viewpoint in order to examine the irrational with his patient. This very detachment appeared almost a lack of moral fiber in the doctor. Seeing a child coming to school in midwinter in shirtsleeves, unfed, we wondered who would step in to issue some directives. The doctor did not judge these crises as we did and would avoid telling parents what to do. He would attempt to keep out of their pathology and the possibility of angry retaliation. He looked at his job as that of understanding the meaning of any particular incident in terms of the total personality of his patient. Since we assumed that the student must appear in the same light to him as he did to us we expected the doctor to worry the way we did and to act!

We were almost always the ones to act in initiating calls to psychotherapists and this put us in the classical position of turning to the doctor—who really knows best, really is in charge. By appealing to him a position of deference was emphasized. In general status terms the teacher is less important, less powerful, less of an authority than the doctor. Both call themselves professionals, but teachers often are insecure in their professional function. They do not enjoy the respect which doctors command from the community and have little independence of action compared to physicians. While we as teachers were free of many of the organizational constraints usually operating in a school system we were still more tied down by the nature of our work than doctors and we felt the common attitude of their assumed superiority. We could be easily reached while they could rarely be telephoned directly. Therapy hours were not to be disturbed but classroom work could be interrupted. Something of the prima donna and the drudge emerged in the relationship as the magical and special realm of the doctor contrasted painfully with the plain, workaday, visible sphere of the teacher.

Perhaps in school situations where the teacher is absolute leader of the class and the students are treated as those who must follow it is not so difficult for that teacher to take the part of a student with a psychiatrist. In our school the teacher-student relationship was very different and it strengthened our own desire to be treated as equals by doctors. We tried to answer any and all questions about our students and ourselves in order to give the doctor the fullest picture possible. We rarely felt reciprocity and although we realized that because of the confidential nature of the therapeutic relationship there were constraints upon the doctor we still believed that there could have been more sharing.

When the school closed we asked several of the psychotherapists who had treated RSS students to discuss with us the particular learning problems of their patients and the relevance of RSS to them. We also wanted to talk about dealing with parents and distinctions between teaching and therapy. Every one of them agreed to meet with us, and all the talks were easy and cordial. They underlined what a variety of interpretations could be made of both student behavior and ours, but also brought forth many areas of correspondence.

The same doctor worked with Jimmy and Larry. He saw Jimmy during the entire time he was with us and for a year or so thereafter. Larry went to him for a short period only, and the doctor knew less about him. He stated that for both boys education had been a major part of the trouble, and though both had received special help and attention in their earlier schools, academic and behavioral problems worsened.

Referring to Larry, the doctor was quick to minimize his own part in helping the boy. He thought that family secrets together with an overwhelming fear of both his own aggressive feelings and those of others were the two themes of Larry's case. The unusual story of the hidden relationships of the children to the adults in Larry's family would be enough in itself to validate the family secrets origin of his school failure. Added to this were the dubious "businesses" of his stepfather and his associates. Larry's fears of what knowledge might lead to were also grounded in the severe oral deprivation he suffered during his first year of life when his mother was almost too depressed to look at him or touch him. Larry's fear of learning was a phobia of taking anything from the outside—so dangerous because what might grown-ups *not* do?— and learning was letting grown-ups do something to him which he could only perceive as threatening.

The doctor thought we were also therapists for both Jimmy and Larry. He called his own work classical psychotherapy because it was more introspective and removed from the heat of battle. He tried to look at everything that was going on calmly and coolly. In our view Jimmy was an accomplished manipulator and insti-gator within the group. His doctor saw him differently, without that potency, because weaknesses were apt to occupy therapeutic sessions. He did think that Jimmy, identifying with us, saw himself rescuing children. Near the end of our work with Jimmy, we learned he had become active in assisting local highway police who patrolled the highways. His doctor interpreted this police work as more rescue activity, rejecting or minimizing the sadistic-authori-tarian impulses we found so evident. To his doctor, Jimmy was a boy making a tremendous effort to form a conscience.

For this doctor, we were on-the-spot workers taking care of the school part of Jimmy's life. Jimmy could get close to us, vent his anger, without fear of consequences. Jimmy thought that all we cared about was that he learn. The doctor added that Marilyn was one woman to whom Jimmy could be close without threat of sur-gery or some other ruin! Apparently Jimmy did not express nega-tive reactions about us in therapy and regarded us as valuable supports throughout.

The doctor praised our allowing freedom without indulgence. In his opinion, parents were the crucial people to scrutinize when deciding how to help kids like Jimmy and Larry. He was changing his emphasis from concentration on the careful screening of the child to critical evaluation of the parents of the prospective young patient. He found that a child who looked very sick at first might have a much better prognosis if he had parents determined to hold on to him and work out some way of living together. Conversely a child who looked healthier and who even might be healthier when referred, did not move forward or perhaps became even sicker despite treatment, because the parents were really backing away, giving no trust. Such parents pulled their children out one way or another when those helping them began to get somewhere. This doctor was most emphatic that from his viewpoint both Jimmy and Larry were in very bad shape when we took them on, and yet with all their problems, the families of both boys had the qualities he had found necessary for real change. He thought, for example, that Jimmy's father, for all his castrating drive, had been surprising in his ability to trust the doctor and the special school. Jimmy was a proven example of a successful course of treatment at RSS, the best example one could offer. The doctor didn't agree with us when we told him that we considered Larry to have been our triumph of triumphs.

According to this doctor, our insistence on Jimmy's treating us as teachers instead of parental surrogates was very valuable, as was our help in defining for the boy the differences between his therapy and our school. Separation of teacher and parent as well as separation of teacher and therapist put the student in greater control of his situation, which was all to the good. If this left the student free to manipulate and juggle a bit, he thought this helped to develop his strength. However, our disapproval of Jimmy's sly manipulations was based on moral scruple.

The doctor thought the "spanking" Larry got at RSS was a turning point in the work. Larry feared what others might do to him, and to see an adult he liked act out his frustration without actually annihilating him was the most reassuring thing that could have happened in school. After that, Larry felt safe with us, and he could begin discovering—or rather, uncovering—and then build up solidly. Before that Larry's only really safe relationships were with animals.

Amy's doctor also worked with Matt and Alden. He thought of learning as a normal stage of development which comes after the oedipal phase. For him, it is part of sublimation, and every culture recognizes its importance, though not necessarily through schools. He gave the gastrointestinal analogy, often used to explain learning and said he thought that Amy was a starvation problem. If you are starving and need to starve for certain psychological reasons, you can't take in learning. Amy's psychological reasons were connected with sexual problems she had about her father who took the role of teacher in the family. It was his practice at home to gather all his children around the table and expect a high level of performance, sneering sarcastically when one failed to be "bright." With this background, Amy's doctor thought that school was irrelevant for her at the time she was with us, that she had come to RSS prematurely. Yet he regarded us as invaluable because without us Amy might have required hospitalization. He continued to see her regularly for a long time, and he said she was now better able to learn and had been doing so until preparations for her recent wedding became intense. He predicted she would improve as a learner. But he added that she had never become completely involved with us because we were "outsiders" and not "upper class" enough.

The coolness we had always felt in her was her way of saying that we didn't really count. He pointed out that Amy had a lot of conflict about this and thought our criticism of her social snobbery made her choose between the school's values and those of her mother. He said that taking her to a public school was really a punishment in her eyes, and by preparing her to go from RSS to public school we had set up a situation she could not tolerate. That was why she left us before we had finished. Yet the doctor considered our work with her a great success. He accounted for our good relationship with her parents on the ground that they did not consider RSS a school at all, but as a signal recognition that Amy could not learn. He added that our holding Amy responsible for her own development was reassuring to them as well.

Alden ended his therapy soon after leaving RSS. The doctor's final impression of Alden was, like ours, that he had been somehow cut loose from life and was just drifting. Their last contact had taken place when Alden and his mother considered his return to some school, though both knew it would be useless since Alden

could not study. The doctor had advised the family to let the boy
go to work, but he detected a worry about the draft behind their
hesitations.

The doctor described Alden as a boy whose mother and father
had school problems, too. The father had had to change colleges,
and the mother having submitted for years to home tutoring left
college in her freshman year, unable to endure the pressure.
Alden's mother had always complained that she could not "get to"
her son. The doctor said it was as if Alden turned everyone into
his mother, and then removed himself so he could not be touched.
Alden had done this even to his therapist, who said he was baffled
and could not make a relationship with the boy. He thought
Alden had used us both as objects rather than people. We served
him by helping him get his own way, and as long as that went on,
it was good. While we appeared as an ally against his parents,
Alden would cooperate, but when we crossed him there was only
bitterness and enmity. The doctor saw this as an infantile way of
viewing the "good daddy and mommy." Oddly enough, the doctor
thought we had been more help to the parents than to the child,
because we held Alden responsible, lifting the burden from them.
This was like the situation with Amy's parents. He described
Alden's relationship with us as strange "melding" from which
Alden did not separate himself enough to make two whole persons. So it looked as if Alden took on RSS only for use in a war
against his parents.

Little was said about Matt because his doctor insisted the moment was not propitious to reveal pertinent information. He said
he would go over Matt's work with us after Matt had struggled
through a current family crisis. This doctor often talked freely of
failures, but perhaps since Matt's going to college was an unquali-
fied success, he did not feel inclined to discuss it. Matt's doctor
said the kids used us as parents, but we definitely had kept our
identities as teachers. That we were a man and a woman made the
parent role unavoidable, but even when we served as parents, our
teaching role persisted. In psychotherapy one would work on
everything else and let the learning come eventually by itself. We
teachers identified problems for the students in order to push
them aside. Our focus, he said, was on academic learning. He

added that what we did was a function of each of us as personalities and not part of a "planned job."

He thought it important for parents to hear from us and not from social workers or other intermediaries how we held the child responsible for his predicament. The parents needed to know from us that we appreciated what qualities in their child had been irritating them for so long. Yet he said that parents usually did not want to change themselves and he thought we should have seen them only when they were interfering with the progress of the child. He thought in the adolescent group it would have been all right to keep the parents at arm's length. This doctor's parting shot was that none of the kids he had sent us was really "ready" to come to school for none had reached the learning stage of human development.

The therapists generally agreed that working with parents was our most serious difficulty. It was their belief that we involved ourselves too intensely. In making children choose sides we imposed too heavy a burden. Happy that we offered students a steady point of view, the therapists stressed the weakness of their patients and recoiled before our strongly expressed opinions and categorical judgments. We could not have been as detached as they without sacrificing an idea of commitment we sought to build into our students.

What are we to conclude about our relationships with the psychotherapists? Obviously they were unsatisfactory from our point of view and at least some of the doctors expressed their own discontent. It is our impression that the problem is a widespread one and that generally teachers and psychiatrists do not communicate well nor work together profitably despite the best of intentions. They appear capable of appreciating the worth of each other's work, both intent upon promoting learning through problem solving. However, the nature of the problems to be solved, the level at which they are approached, the structure within which they are treated, and the role of the professional person attempting their solution are different enough to create a considerable separation. Are the differences too great to bridge? Are the relationships so poor because there is little ground for building between them?

How meaningful is the concept of the team approach in this area?

Sheer lack of knowledge has certainly exacerbated the difficulties in what transpires between psychiatrists and teachers. Stepping back from our own work it is hard to miss the message that the issues could have been made far clearer between us. Whether or not that clarity could then have served as a basis for more productive relationships is not certain. That it would have cleared the air of a good many petty frustrations seems surer. As it was, the ambiguities of an almost totally unstructured situation led to the formation of ridiculously stereotypic pictures of one another. These impressions led to unrealistic expectations. The doctors tended to rely upon images of us as seen through the eyes of colleagues who had sent children to our school or as portraits painted by patients. No matter how thoroughly corrected the latter may have been by the doctor's knowledge of his patient's distortions it is hard to see how a real picture could have been transmitted. We, in our narrowness, relied upon Marilyn's background in psychiatric social work and the fact that she was married to a psychiatrist to reveal to us what all psychiatrists were doing. She leaned too heavily upon her personal knowledge of individual doctors and so we were often without adequate information about their theories and methods of practice and about their attitudes toward school and teachers. Because she herself had done psychotherapy with children in the past she generalized too broadly from that experience. Her change of roles had changed her far more than she then understood.

In the end the relationships which are worked out will always depend upon the particular combinations of people and circumstances involved. There appears to be no overriding rule which could have been applied to meet successfully all the combinations which emerged in our years of RSS. What we might have proposed to each doctor was a kind of contact which did not need to involve confidences; in fact the therapist could have been largely free to write his own terms, even to the point of saying that he did not wish to have any exchange at all. As teachers we needed only to know what his conditions were; whether or not to send regular reports to him; whether he wanted to give us advice; whether he would arrange for emergency appointments if we recommended them; whether he would acknowledge or comment upon our reports. Of course we preferred the idea of working together as fully as possible and most of the therapists seeing our students agreed that we should. Explicit terms of cooperation would be only the beginning of an ideal relationship between teachers and therapists. It is clear that they have much to learn from each other about work with troubled and failing students.

IX ❦ *Failure and Success*

TOILING ALONG THE RSS road, students found a way to escape learning disabilities. If they kept to the route as marked, they returned successfully to regular schools; many went on to college. They became not more manageable, but more teachable.

Reading disorders got the bulk of remedial attention and were usually the first to be retired. Yet we could not measure such progress with "objective" certainty. Scores from the periodically given standardized achievement tests had only the superficial value of grade placement. Except in the face of primitive illiteracy, we avoided the isolation of the so-called techniques of reading. No student at RSS was allowed to fall back on those mechanical devices or on the timed, graded reading exercises that lard orthodox remedial programs in the hope of quick evidence of "progress." Such drills, in the name of training eyes to be ever more agile, commit the kind of spiritual murder that had already confirmed our students in their disaffection with reading and studying. The slow, inept reader got along at RSS without words-per-minute or multiple-choice "comprehension" checks. He plunged, instead, into the task of more consciously organizing his thoughts and feelings about what he read, wading into the unconditioned heart of intelligent human learning.

Adolescents are generally preoccupied with the age-old personal problems which accompany civilized growth. Our students were exaggeratedly concerned. They concentrated on the more violent human emotions and actions which, in imagination, lead destructively to mayhem, murder, and rape; they speculated about retributions attending such crimes. Their "secret" literature and off-the-record conversations indicated a train of thought dominated by sexual connotations. It is futile to moralize or say what their minds ought to have been thinking. On the other hand, when they discovered their secret thoughts had long been in the public domain through the literary work of Sophocles, Euripides, Homer, and Shakespeare, they were shocked. They were astonished by incest in *Oedipus Rex*, child slaughter and female vindictiveness in *Medea*, ambition and murder in *Macbeth*, blood baths and treachery in the *Iliad*, and unprincipled craftiness in the *Odyssey*. Reading over these works, students learn that their hoarded feelings and private fantasies are part of the common fabric of human experience. They find that when dread events, in which they can recognize their worst feelings, have called forth nobility, courage, and even pity, they can enter the substance of the highest human drama and penetrate the most moving literature. Reading *is*, then, thinking and feeling!

The technical difficulties of Shakespeare are not insurmountable for poor readers. The challenge often brings quick improvements. Good recent translations of the Greek tragedies are technically easy for anyone able to read at all. Modern works like the short stories of Pushkin, Katherine Mansfield, and Kafka, offer similar opportunities. Arthur Miller's *Death of a Salesman* proved so moving an experience that students who had never wanted to see or read a play, wept openly. This new dimension for hitherto private worlds pointed the way to a reading success which, springing from moral and artistic choices, is still remote from a world measured in test scores.

Escape from writing disabilities through aesthetic experiences proved far more difficult. Compositions eked out in class were masses of mangled spelling, punctuation, and syntax. Worse, they were models of artificiality and boring respectability. Almost the only honest sentiment expressed was a loathing for all required writing. Bad experiences, real or imagined, had brought them to believe that genuine self-expression inspired punishment, and honest communication left them open to adult manipulative controls. One student wrote the position out clearly:

I will not be able to write any more for you even though

sometimes you make me want to write. The reason is that if I write again, it will give you a way to get your lever into my mind. Then you would begin to pry it open. I cannot let you in.

After trust was established we could begin the long trek through an alphabetical wilderness. Writing well does, in most instances, require both a well-digested and a good reading background. This partially explains why few adolescents can be taught grammar and spelling if they have not already mastered these "skills" by the end of grammar school. Remedial schools may spend many hours drilling and remedial teachers do ceaselessly argue the virtues of one system over another, but the informality of English grammar seems to require that it be instilled at home with the beginning of speech itself; schools can only help a student convert what he already knows into generalizations which he can more consciously apply to new fields. Good spelling is even more elusive than grammar; accuracy depends upon unique combinations of experience and calculation, delicate blendings of learning factors easily ruined by even slight disaffections. While our students generally improved their writing enough to satisfy the regular schools and colleges to which they went, we remained unimpressed with the level of their writing achievements at RSS.

Except for math and other "subject-matter" courses, there was no simple gauge of "improved skills" that provided a reliable guide in evaluating progress. We had only occasional glimpses of encouraging technical changes in reading and writing; because RSS was special we could only guess what individuals might do in the face of the "normal" tensions and trials that formerly disabled them. The test lay in the regular classroom—outside our province. Nevertheless, after six months of intensive work we were so close to our students that if they did not actually tell us, we usually intuitively knew what decisions they were ready to make. For practical purposes we had to determine their grade levels, but the more important evaluations were unnumbered conjectures in terms of maturity and independence. If our students could find their own direct ways to express dissent and if, in consequence, they could accept the teacher's authority, understanding its limits and uses, we were willing to predict that they would be able to solve their technical problems easily, quickly, and more or less on their own.

🦚

"You two make me more depressed and sad than ever when you try to get me to talk about my failure, and my only defense is to get snotty and bitchy," says Alden.

"I know I'm wrong, but it's hopeless," says Franny.

"My only regret is that I was born," says Tom.

"Nobody can ever make it up to me," says Amy.

"I feel like a rat in a trap when I end up on your side," says Ned.

"I agree with you for my own reasons, but if I admit it, they'll say I'm brown-nosing," says Jimmy.

"If I get all this taken care of now, how'll I get along next year when I won't have you?" says Matt.

Even Amy and Tom now know we are on their side, and naturally enough they all look around for someone else to blame. The developing sense of responsibility points inward, and though this be the start of reconstruction, the road ahead looks dismally long and difficult. Exaggerating his insolvency, the student turns on himself the anger hitherto directed against teachers and parents. Self-blame, added to self-doubt and self-pity, intensifies despair, and for a time he feels his case is hopeless. Declaring his need at last, he is greedy for our support and begs for more, only to recoil in terror, remembering ancient fears of domination and manipulation. His faith in us which has taken a headlong leap into the open is obscured by spasmodic retreats into depression and doubt. His fantasies about our motives come and go, but the comfort and strength he derives from unashamed dependence on us begin to mean more to him than his fears. He starts to embrace our precepts and breaks away from disability toward competence and freedom.

Our developing relationships bring new crises in which we are more personally involved than ever. The student sometimes wishes dreamily that we could adopt him, wrap him up, and bring him in out of the storm. After working so long without credit, we find ourselves basking in a new admiration and indeed in some ways we do "adopt" him. We feel tender and generous when we see him suffering, angry and disgusted when he treats us badly or regresses unpleasantly. We are heartened by sudden outbursts of courage and unexpected gleams of intelligence when he examines his own defeat. We are inspired and touched when he thinks us infallible.

Tempting as it may be we do not want him to picture us deprived of our shortcomings or eternally devoted to his service. We bring it home that we are not, nor will we be obligated to these children as parents. We are not going to endure every sacrifice to help them, and moreover find ourselves driven to acknowledge defeat when they ask for too much. At this point, time and again students veer around and return to course, steady and willing. They call on unused resources when they see ours withdrawing and appreciate what we give them when we refuse to waste it. We must protect our identity as teachers to prevent them from backsliding. Of course we would fail if we did not stand firm as friends, but we would be questionable friends if we lost our integrity as teachers.

A few cannot set much store by our understanding and sympathy. Some consider our help only a down payment on what they intend to collect from a world that cheats them of an essential birthright. They dedicate their adolescence to one-sided bookkeeping, allowing nothing to displace the primacy of their own selfishness. Our personal needs do not impress them for they have no power realistically to perceive the needs of egos other than theirs. They scrutinize us merely to determine which of our acts nourish their covetousness and which are part of a "plot" to hurt them. Blindness to the benefits of mutuality makes them inaccessible to us.

Our failure with Amy is a great disappointment because so many factors are in her favor. Her intelligence is high; her therapist approves of our dealings with her and talks with us often; her relationship with him is good, and she tries to work her way out of her psychological difficulties; though her parents have grave problems to which Amy's are closely linked, her mother and father are perceptive, psychologically sophisticated, and ready to do what they can to help. But Amy stubbornly plays out the part of a de-

prived, neglected, hapless waif. She is wise enough to show deference when prudence dictates, but an imperious willfulness does
not allow her to respect us as teachers or friends with whom she
dares be honestly herself. She preys upon us and withholds herself with brutal disregard for the consequences of her ceaseless
feeding. Her therapist sees this situation as potentially beneficial,
but to us it smacks too much of the kind of custodial care we
despise. Besides, it will not get her back to regular school, and so
we say in our midyear report. We are making no headway in
securing a commitment to academic learning, although she has
become candid enough to abandon spurious claims to interest in
various subjects.

With the approval of her doctor we invite the family to look
realistically at our failure to help, and to consider how to go about
finding a different setting for her. Amy opposes us and insists her
feelings about school have really changed. She is just getting ready
to get down to work, she says, and with a little more time everything will be all right. Knowing well enough her heart has not
changed, we are still swayed by her labored eagerness to make it
change, for we are loath to give her up. Amy's parents being wiser
than we in the ways of their daughter are also more skeptical, but
they too want to give her another chance. At their request we set
up a program of fortnightly checkup meetings to review Amy's
work, deciding each time whether to go on for another two weeks.
On the face of it this kind of emergency handling is effective. Amy
rouses her disheveled and amorphous self and stops signing her
compositions "Little Amy." Her moods are still capricious, but less
profound, and she seems to make more effort to control her
behavior when depressed, participating more alertly in classwork
and discussions. Scrounging at lunch time and habitual tardiness
are warning signals, but we are satisfied that she is earning the
right to finish out the year with us.

After we drop the emergency meetings, events outside school
deepen her moodiness, and psychological preoccupations domi-
nate once again. She balks at serious efforts to discriminate between what can best be aired in school and what reserved for
psychotherapy. She and her therapist sometimes consider us
custodial adjuncts, though she would add the convenience of hav-

ing us do therapy too, because knowing us better she sometimes
would rather talk to us. But erotic and other fantasies have no
place in RSS. We do discuss measures to get around such disturbances for the sake of studying and learning. When she gives
us a hint we decide whether it is a school problem. If it is not,
she telephones her doctor for an emergency appointment. Sometimes it is enough to talk with him on the telephone. She may
walk around the block; if necessary she may take the whole day
off. She can arrange to stay after school and talk with us as a
friend or comrade. But Amy will not rely on these constructive,
nonsuppressive measures to delay the urgency of deep psychological problems. She argues that they have to be *solved* before she
can study. When we ask whether being in therapy exempts her
from every decision and action, she turns back to her books and
seems to study.

As the year nears its close together we lay plans for her return
to regular high school. It is doubtful that she will be able to
handle it, but she says she can and asks our backing. At her request Marilyn accompanies her to the interview with the high
school principal. Amy is well-groomed and in wonderful spirits.
She makes a favorable impression on the principal, and carries off
the interview with great success. The next day we are ready to
congratulate her, and the other students are set up too. She is the
first of the group to move out into the world where they must
all go sooner or later, and her victory encourages and gladdens
them. But where is she? At ten o'clock she sidles into her seat looking like a rumpled laundry pile. She smiles absently but says
nothing in reply to our praise or to the general conversation about
her achievement. She hates it! At the break she steals Jimmy's
lunch, and wolfs it down without a word. Replying to our surprised indignation, she unleashes hidden fury in a gross, violent,
and spiteful tantrum. She refuses pointblank to discuss anything
further with us, and walks out the door never to return as a
student.

It shocks us deeply, and shatters the others who immediately
demand to know whether they too will collapse at the first breath
from outside.

The hesitation, doubt, and last-minute panicky unwillingness that all our students face at the end of our work together do not account for Amy's defection. The positive direction of real events forces her to reveal that she does not want a formal education. Behind her anger lies deep disappointment in her parents; she identifies their excellent and successful educational backgrounds with those psychological difficulties that impede worldly efficiency and interfere with the flow of giving she wants from them. Her mother's assumption of family power hits Amy as a loss to herself; she fears that academic success will make her overcompetent, domineering, and hard, that is, unfeminine like her mother.

On leaving RSS Amy takes a training course in a secretarial school and has a brief career as a secretary. Two years later she comes to visit Marilyn and me in our homes to see whether we will approve her fiancé. She consults our moral judgment, for she is marrying a man whose political ambitions may lead her to violate her conscience by condoning racial inequality in the South. When she invites us to her wedding, she includes us in an intimate group of close friends and family; starting her new life, she wants us to know our work is not in vain.

When Alden's great crisis comes, he too renounces his academic potential and turns away from us, a default which is no surprise. The incident is trivial but the issue is not. An accident puts his car in the repair shop and he begins driving to school in his girl's car without permission from his parents. We disapprove of his driving anyway, and think this underhanded disobedience fraught with complications monopolizing his attention when we want it. Alden is not to be persuaded, so at last we lay down the law and forbid him to come to school unless he uses his own family's car or the MTA. The issue is drawn, and we wonder whether the relationship he has built with us and his progress toward a return to school will mean enough to him. Can he give in to our demands and give up a willful excursion? The answer is a quick, thumping, "No!" He readily abandons all he has won in school to avoid the inconvenience of public transportation. He is so furious at our attempt to limit his will that he keeps away even after his own car is back in commission. He is through, and not only with us; he stops going to his therapist at the same time. He will submit to no schedule, no obligation, no requirement when it clashes with his caprice.

Alden's doctor has never established a reciprocal relationship with him. Years ago when he had been called on for help, he stepped in and went to bat for Alden to abate the severity of parental punishment. Alden still turns to him for this service, but has little understanding of the therapist's real role. Other people and things are in like manner used to satisfy immediate, usually sensual, impulses for pleasure, and Alden quickly disavows the sources of satisfaction so as to escape responsibility. In this basic refusal to carry on a human relationship, we are brought face to face with chaotic and destructive feelings which skulk behind the conformist urbanity of Alden's parents. In fact we find Alden exploding with those feelings his parents could not act out for themselves. The family scorns teachers and others who work for a living without making much money. Truth-telling itself becomes wicked and lower class where the fabric of banal conventionality and social snobbery, supported by a large unearned income, "excuses" an irresponsible, willful lack of seriousness. In the context of conformity we are easily made to look out of place and in the wrong. Our failure only pleases them, for if we, the last of the experts, cannot hold Alden to any rational obligation, we give—as they think—the final license to youthful disorder.

Alden leaves school, gives up his therapy, and simply stays home. He has joined his parents in proving that he is beyond help, and this leads to some sort of peace between them. His mother calls in the summer to ask Marilyn to tutor him in a home-study program, but later we hear no more about it. Alden rests for a while, and then takes a job as a helper in a nearby graveyard. Over a year later we get in touch with his parents to ask them to talk to us about their views of our work. We are amazed at their friendliness and eagerness to cooperate with our project. Alden makes a special trip in to see us and review the past. He is more judicious and less passionate than we remember, and talks about definite plans for going to a preparatory school. He says he is grateful to us for making him see that he cannot submit to us, or to any orderly, rational obligation. He says he decided to quit RSS on that issue, and now is dealing with it in a nonacademic setting. Working as an apprentice gardener, he thinks he may be dissolving his resistance to authority and self-discipline. If he does go to school again, he adds, he will accept obligation in advance. We suppose he is sporting a new set of clichés. He is an academic loss.

Tom likes RSS. His attachment to Jimmy and Matt draws him toward acceptance of it. Envious of their growing freedom he tries to imitate them, but he misses the point, for he refuses to find out as they have done, how to express freely, regularly, and verbally the feelings that interfere with learning. He cannot follow us further without a collision with his father, and his fear of reprisals from that quarter remains uppermost, eroding the simple beginnings of his trust in us. He never relinquishes his long-practiced misrepresentations and disguises, and so only goes through the motions of studying without the least ability to concentrate or learn.

We try to persuade his father to be more tolerant of RSS. We write letters and meet with him to promote a better understanding, and we recommend a consultation with a psychotherapist of his own choice. We point out that for the first time in Tom's school life he has no respiratory attacks requiring anti-allergy pills that make him drowsy and dull, that his mind thus liberated can be sharp and clear. He has shown an order of intelligence which ought to end their doubts of his capacity. This argues, we say, that RSS has a school atmosphere in harmony with his needs and conducive to his growth. We ask for parental support in our efforts to bring out Tom's feelings; we fear that otherwise his reaction to the strain of divided loyalties will be sullen and more intractable. We appeal to the father to release the son before it is too late. Listening impatiently, the father shows how unalterably opposed he is to psychological investigation or treatment of learning problems. He says there is no scientific proof of psychotherapeutic cures and as a scientist he will not rely on them. He does agree to an outside consultation. The doctor to whom he turns makes no effort to talk to us or hear about our experience with Tom. He endorses the father's pessimistic outlook and likewise sees no help for Tom in psychotherapy. They nevertheless wish the boy to continue with us.

We must now take a stand. If we persist with the measures we believe in we will cause severe and bootless suffering; if we follow the father's wishes, we will become neutral custodians. Neither option will help with the learning problems, so we request the family to withdraw Tom from school.

As we see it, Tom's domineering father is postponing his son's approaching manhood. In disappointment or in fear, this father pegs his son as a weakling and dullard who will not be able—or allowed—to follow in his footsteps. After leaving RSS Tom often comes to see Marilyn. Limp and unannounced on her doorstep, he is eager to talk with her, and tags along on household errands. Sometimes he arrives with a friend to whom he introduces her with great pride. Tom is now a wanderer among marginal boarding and day schools, a confused misfit unable to learn with full intelligence, chaotically approaching a tragic future. We do not really understand the irrational forces ruling his life, but we believe that he might have succeeded at RSS with the help of psychotherapy.

Franny's potential had been considered low, like Tom's, but the difference here is that her family wants it to be high—indeed requires it to be. At first Franny seems chronically tense in academic settings. Primordial guilt mechanisms appear to command her personality, egging her into outward and visible motions of learning while her inner self runs for cover, weeping and cursing. She is convinced that learning is a mechanical process to be turned on whilst her thinking and feeling self stands aside, either in opposition or without interest. It takes most of the year for us to secure a variation in this pattern. She learns to say "no," but her initial refusals are angry bursts of resistance rather than sources of relief or understanding; they do not thaw out the interior though tears do flow more often. The question is: How can she change her inner style when the debacles that hound her from day to day lead her to believe that academically she *must* fail, and all her choices seem to lead to the same hopeless defeat!

Meanwhile, in Franny's home, the anxiety of a perfectionist mother is only gradually subsiding; yet this is the change upon which Franny's chances hang. Her mother still expects us to use conventional exercises and drills to bring Franny up to snuff. She does not understand our explanations, for our ideas are too unfamiliar to sink in. She listens with deaf ears, hearing only what she expects. When Franny suddenly begins to tax her with being an overbearing, interfering mother she sails in to scold us. She threatens to withdraw Franny, raging like a wounded lioness except that instead of roaring, she telephones. I explain our ideas again, hopeful of her interest, but it is a tedious process and sometimes I speak impatiently. She is less scandalized by my retorts than by my insistence on keeping Franny informed about these phone calls. She manages Franny's affairs by operating behind the scenes though nothing really confidential is at stake. It may never occur to her that Franny has a right to know. Her first step forward is to grant recognition to her daughter; seeing Franny as a person for the first time, her mother begins to consult her. We send detailed reports home and meet with both parents frequently, and sometimes we seem to work as hard with them as with Franny. Though unable to change much in school, she is asserting herself effectively at home. At first alarmed, her mother now finds this attitude creates unexpected harmony in the family. She renews efforts to understand us in terms of her own scheme of values. Her excessive organizing diminishes with the decline of fears about Franny's being accepted in the world. Feeling more independent, Franny studies with a little more heart. But alas, her reading and spelling are as bad as ever, for making headway against her mother's pressure brings disappointingly little improvement to her academic work.

Daily struggle with Franny does not reach well-defined crises. Direct confrontation proves too radical for her conservative soul, for she cannot throw her conventions to the winds and stand on the platform of her self, and there is no use forcing.

We are at odds on so many points that Franny's invitation to the school comes as a pleasant surprise. She says her mother and father would like us to hold our closing-day picnic at their house. Two months ago it would have been impossible to imagine Matt's bearded face or Larry's South Boston accent being welcome on their manicured suburban lawn. We accept cheerfully but as the time approaches we see our mistake. Franny is relaying her *mother's* invitation. Barbed remarks about last-minute arrangements make it clear that she disassociates herself from the plan. We are on the spot, for we cannot go to her house unless she is the one to invite us—though a sudden reversal will surely dampen the good spirits our closing day should promote. While all are sitting in the front room, we announce our withdrawal. The students are disappointed, and Franny looks crushed. It is a crisis we cannot put off. We tell the group that we are willing to go, but only if Franny invites us. It is a terrible moment for Franny; she wants to invite us but cannot bring herself to do it. She sits in her chair coloring deeply and weeping, but can only shake her head. Though we understand her attitude, it is insulting, and so we tell her. She begins to recognize the spreading, destructive effect of her resentment against her mother's interference. At last she admits she does want us to come, and despite her grudging manner, we accept. This closing-day picnic is one of the best we ever had.

In the fall Franny's return to her old school is disheartening. We think she has changed too little to do well in any regular school, and certainly she ought not to go where her worst feelings will revive. However we are wrong, as we discover months later when her mother comes to visit and tells us with tears in her eyes how Franny has been living through a severe crisis, facing her most difficult school problems, and coming around at last to a positive feeling about school. As we knew she would, Franny found the school life intolerable, and complaining of sickness she began staying home. When at last she decided to leave school, she was amazed to find her parents backing her up. They went along with her to the interview in which she confessed tearfully to the headmaster that he frightened her so much she could not stay in his school. Her parents now knew how to stand by as supporters, and the headmaster handled this moment of courage with sudden insight and sympathy. As a result Franny accepted his invitation to come back and try again, and she began to do well in all schoolwork. Her mother confesses now that she fought us at every turn. She says when she and her husband read our first reports they could not understand them. Later, they began to see what we were driving at, and now when some problem comes up they go back and re-read them to refresh their understanding. She grins happily and says that the reports are worn thin with use. She concludes by saying that though we never saw Franny solve her problems at RSS, she wants us to know that Franny has come through because of what she learned with us. Franny herself best confirms her mother's views by at last entering college.

Larry uses many school hours to write the autobiographical sketches in which he learns slowly how to spell and make correct sentences. Most of all he learns about himself. In these writings are merged the currents of nearly all his school problems. Beginning with a fantasy, they speak—and spell—for themselves:

> I govt in my jet and toook ovf with 12 H bomb and bomd 100'000 schools. the firs school I bomd was in Boston. it was fun and I was glad to see it go up in the air. it was my firs school I want to wan I was a child and all the tichers in the school was blowd up in the air and the sacond school was in Cambridge. it was the school I did,t wot to blow up in the air be cos in a way I lict it and the tichers to. and I blowd it up in the air anyway.

In this, his first composition dealing with his thoughts, upside-down commas and apostrophes punctuate his protest, and now his thoughts begin to flow:

> I hate school because the teachers bous me around and I hate it becouse one day woan I was six years old one teacher triad to make me like her and that was it of schools. and No teacher is going to make me like her our he. and I still heer her say *you got to like teachers* and her to. and I'm shoor not going to like thet Jucking teacher. and frther more if thet teacher thinks I'm going to like her shees cracey. and thats sum of my trubl. and ther are too teachers that ar heping me and sum time I don't now how they can stand me.

The conflict between Larry's need to develop in his own way and the adults' will to tame and shape his character is savage and primitive. His retreat is so complete that no teaching technology could find him. He is neither disaffected with the idea of learning nor limited by neurological anomalies, though he seems to be both. Larry's sensitive and alert mind cowers under the impact of organized academic training. He defends himself by staking everything on a refusal to be taught. He wants to learn but he thinks teaching means manipulation. But when he plunges into literacy and reads the *Odyssey*, his imagination takes hold. Unlike many adolescent boys he does not develop that toughness which implies fear of an emotional involvement that would reveal something doubtful about his masculinity. He easily projects his own anger and fear and suffering into what he reads and finds deep meaning and personal satisfaction in literature.

> I enjoyed reading the Odyssey and I hope to read something like it realy soon and there is some thing in the odyssey that I shed a tear for and it was when Odysseus found his wife again after twenty years and that realy got my hart and I had a tear in My eyes when I read that part of the odyssey. and the God that I hatid is the earthshaker and I thought that the earth-shaker was a *God dam bastad* for doing that to odysseus when he was going home.

Larry curses Poseidon, just as he hates teachers, the "gods" who had sabotaged his mind. He fears the force of his own rage against them.

> wen I was a child I yousto hait teachers because one day a long time ago wen I was a child my grandmother brot me to school I was kind ove afraed because I think the teacher didn't lick me because I think she thot I didn't lick her and the principal I think she thot the same thing two. and deep inside I realy whotid to *kill* tim beth, but nawe I'm glad I did't do it. But some times I really whot to kill thim still, and I'm glad I go to school naw but some times I still wish I cod kill thim.

His impulse to kill those teachers of ten years ago is a living force competing even now with his real affection for me as his current teacher. Its urgency grows whenever I attempt direct instruction. It suffuses every corner of what is specifically academic in our relationship. But when at long last he throws his hated workbook against the wall, what sadness lies behind the angry tears that spring into his eyes! He so fears his ungovernable rage will annihilate our relationship if not my person. Compositions allow him to express the feelings safely in words.

Teaching him to spell is doomed to failure. He works diligently; he reviews lists of words and sounds; he uses methods of every sort. The harder we concentrate on it the worse he spells, and the angrier we both get. Even when my "instruction" is at his own request, he unfailingly identifies me with the teacher about whom he had written, "I still heer her say you got to like teachers and her to." His reaction is iterative and unflagging, "I'm shoor not going to like thet Jucking teacher." He strikes back for every smiling overture; hard-pressed, he withdraws completely, repeating stonily, "I don't get it." Outwardly metallic, a real "motor-mouth," a machine that cannot "like" school, his compact fury frightens and enrages the most tenderhearted and well-meaning teachers. He is condemned to renounce his dearest wish, for he still identifies learning with personal submission. He does not and never will like that teacher! Thus illiteracy is rooted in a scruple.

Autobiography suggests a way out:

> I think that I understand a little More of spelling than I did before. and I'm begining to like Writeing shot storeys about My solf and I think it is a lot easier writeing about My solf then talking about things that I couldent discus by talking. and I hope to Write my freinds When I get a little better in Writeing and I know that I have to larn to Spell and I hope to be a good Writer and Speller . . . I feel a lot better after I get my agar out and I can work a little and I whos glad we had that tolk yesterday but at first I did't whet to tolk but in a why I'm glad we did and I think I can work know and I think when I get Mad I will triy to tolk a little two.

Larry lays his ghosts one by one, putting into words the old thoughts and feelings that are to him as if "now." A realization of the true sequence of events helps him control his self-defeating reflexes. His anger, fusing past and present for him, consumes itself.

> I think Mrs. B is a very atractive woman but she is a God dam teacher and I don't like teachas but she is divarent I dont know wiy but I think she is a pretty good teacher and I must be going crasey for saing that to a teacher but I mean that and I think I'm not so mad at teachas but I do have a lot Mor laft . . . I wos glad I didn't have to go to school yesterday because yov got me pretty mad the day bee four

and I whas reely glad I didn't go to school. but the day bie four yasterday whan I whs mad at Mrs. bee for saing That to Me I whs Just furious and I didn't what to say anything about it and I think she did get me reading a littil better and she did go me a littil skid to.

It is a long road, made almost impassable by the intellectual limitations of illiteracy. Larry, largely unfamiliar with concepts, has the greatest difficulty in drawing inferences from familiar facts. The drills and exercises which usually provide the experience necessary for induction are ineffective. His conceptual world is too primitive and disconnected to allow him to progress slowly and easily. He has to make leaps which depend upon a concentrated will power and confidence in us. Sometimes we force these leaps. Despite the high charge of his emotional reactions, when our withdrawal seems imminent, he jumps, grudgingly but satisfactorily.

I like to do a little homework but my T.V. don't want me to and I try not to but my t v wons all most every time but *letly* I'm ben winning and my T.V. hasint and I know thet sometimes my T.V. will win but only when I'm mad. I hop I wont get mad very much now and I hop thet I can win the war betwin me and the TV . . . When my father gets mad at me I feel pretty bad about it. Because I what to pleas him instead of getting him mad at me. But sometimes we get in a ergyoument and thet sats the firecrecker off and so We fite. Like ferinstens I got in a fite with My Mother about raking the yard but I don't like to do it and so I stold by saying I'll do it in an hour and so she fargets all that day and so I don't do it. But When she asks me a gen then I say I don't what to do it. the We get in a fite and so she tells Dad on me and so We get in a God dam fite a gen and I hate them. But there is one thing I hate and it is When I fite with My father over My Mother's problm with me doing things around the yard. it is When we get in a fite I can't say a thing and if I do start to say something he say to me to *keep* quiet and thet gets me furious. and so I get mader at my father. But I still like the old goat just the same.

Larry's whole appearance is changed as if feeding his mind and developing it were the touchstone setting in motion physical forces waiting to be released. His hangdog expression gives way to a look of thoughtfulness and sensitivity. He is handsome and carries himself in a contained way suggesting fulfillment rather than isolation and fear. His silence, once a clamp over urges to kill and devour, changes into reserved sensibility and civilized good manners. Though we know how to deal with his problems, we do not escape them and must work around his rages in every subject we teach. Swift development of his reasoning and conceptual powers is cumulative, however, and he picks up speed every time he passes another obstacle. At last he can make good use of Marilyn's help even though she is a woman teacher. She still rouses angry flurries, but he trusts her almost as much as me.

Larry's parents, with little formal education themselves, do not theorize about his problems. He is turning out to be more of a student than they thought possible and though they never discuss family problems or tell us anything of Larry's past, they give us patient and wholehearted trust for the present. They are, however, disappointed with the slower process of psychotherapy, and after an independent medical consultation, discontinue it. With us Larry takes the initiative in talking about feelings that block him. He is earnest, intelligent, and ultimately successful. There is now little chance for his resuming treatment, though we would like to recommend it. His development suggests that there are students who must solve learning problems *before* they can profit much from psychotherapy.

A year later, Larry entered the ninth grade in a local high school, carrying a full load of academic subjects. Receiving grades high enough for the honor role, Larry has graduated. He had a part in the annual school play, and was frequently consulted by fellow students needing help with schoolwork. Teachers are now among his allies and friends, and they in turn think him so reliable that they entrust their own cars to him. He even comes to call on the hated Mrs. B! Unsympathetic or antagonistic teachers no longer throw him because he busies himself finding reasons for their feelings.

While concentrating on these school achievements, he is jolted anew by family tragedies. His father and mother separate and seem headed for divorce. Just as Larry is getting adjusted to this drastic change, his world is shattered by the sudden death of his mother. Coming to tell us of these events, he talks tearfully of doubts and deep discouragement; of the kindness of a neighbor to whom he blurted out his wish to end it all; of memories of his mother and her hopes for him; and of a calmer determination to serve those memories by finishing the education she herself longed for him to have.

Literacy is not a solution to his psychological problems, but we are satisfied with the direction of his thinking when he writes:

> I like Books know and I like to read them a lot and I like to got to a Bookstore and look at the Books and try to fine a good Book that I might like to read and sometimes when I get mad I like to go in a Bookstore.

Jimmy decides to continue with us but he wants to be forced. Too passive to root out the saboteur inside, he still promotes petty conspiracies against school and teachers. Yet, the quality of his schoolwork is improving every day.

His anti-school behavior is anachronistic, and must be ended. We soon see our chance. One day he calls in to report himself "too sick" to leave home. A moment later Tom telephones with the same complaint. Then, Jimmy's mother, thinking him at school, calls to tell him his lunch is still on the kitchen table at home. Jimmy has betrayed himself. The two boys are truant. Because we have been through the distrust and defiance behind his dishonesty and tricks in school, we feel it right to demand an immediate end to them. In an emergency meeting with Jimmy and his parents we demand that Jimmy either make a clean break with his past in these matters, or pack up his pencils and leave. Jimmy agrees to behave, although he needs a general call to arms to make him act on decisions already taken.

Jimmy has yet to resolve his family difficulties, and he still consults us about his father's attacks. But even if domestic affairs remain a source of anguish, the strong and often loving feelings within his family do contribute to the positive solution of his school problems. His therapist is actively helping him with the deeper issues underlying his struggles to grow into a man, and also works with us so that together we succeed in providing Jimmy with breathing space and time to concentrate on academic failures.

Jimmy goes from RSS to a small independent preparatory school, where he must toil his way through a rigid, old-fashioned course while deciding whether to go to college. He winces, but thrives on strict, authoritarian teaching. After high school he enrolls in a two-year technical college and at last graduates. Glowing with pride, he rushes over to Marilyn's house to show her his diploma, and then runs out to call long-distance so that I too will hear the good news.

Jimmy continues to plan to manage and deceive people, but he is conscious of what he is about and can examine himself objectively when confused or uncertain. He uses honesty, responsiveness, and serious inquiry to overcome difficulties, even though his values are still "operational."

Potentially a person of lofty ideals, Ned is pragmatically self-centered. When we understand his infantile weakness we hold it at bay long enough for positive, life-preserving impulses to grow and order themselves into a pattern. This means holding him responsible in the face of all opposition. Returning the stolen book is the critical moment when Ned begins to accept responsibility. When he first came to RSS he was consulting a psychologist whom he dropped to use us as therapists. We then insisted on his finding the doctor with whom he is now working. This psychiatrist, pursuing a supportive and permissive course, sometimes disapproves of our demands, but nevertheless backs our pushing to give Ned strength. Ned's parents, though they love him, work against this program. Their cynicism and personal disillusionments are especially corrosive because they are such intelligent and articulate people. Their destructive attitude toward life inhibits Ned's natural impulses, stunts his growth, even frightens him. Beliefs and values mean everything to him, though he cries out against them, and subjects ours to wily and sophisticated attacks. It is unfashionable to think people inherently good, but I feel that Ned is—like others for whom reasoning is a spontaneous way of life. Such men may do evil to themselves and others if they are twisted and thwarted, but goodness and compassion always seem natural in these rare humans. Though they need little instruction, they certainly must have examples.

Ned's innate generosity and goodwill shrivel and die when he approaches personal commitment. Fear of being involved seems to echo betrayals in early life. A quick sense of humor takes the guise of self-observation, only to mask other fears, hostility, and anger. His wonderful gift of reason becomes a tool to divert serious discussions into legalistic labyrinths where content and affect are lost in the pursuit of logical quibbles. His intellectual prowess is frittered away furrowing an arid, lifeless desert. Expecting him to welcome the freedom at RSS, we find him ungraciously misusing and dissipating it. Ned is ready to sink into a somnolent lethargy from which only strong external action can rouse him.

Though he hates authority, we have to establish a set of rules and require him to produce. Narrowing the choices available to him in our daily study schedule, we also restrict the range of matters open to discussion. Opportunities to suspect or capriciously to challenge our motives or exercise his powers of controlling adults are held to a minimum. Though he lashes back at us as insensitive, backward, and even power-mad, dealing with him like an infant begins to work. Embarking on independent schoolwork for the first time, he sets himself the goal of learning algebra.

Ned's high school adds incentive to his study program by promising credit for his work at RSS if he passes their tests; still, progress is erratic. He does algebra homework; yet falls apart over assigned compositions. When we ask for simple and accurate analyses of books, he gives us pretentious psychological interpretations of himself. Though he has had little training in detailed examination of material, the real obstacle is easy reliance on sloppy generalizations. As he begins to trust us, we hate to needle him, for he is more unashamedly the baby who is really hurt when not loved unstintingly or praised uncritically. Fortunately his work in algebra is developing into a real achievement, and turning out page after page of homework, he admits he really enjoys the process of problem-solving and learning. But the continuing shoddiness of his work in English needs censure rather than praise; taken to task for it, he threatens general retreat, luring us to coddle him and overlook his shortcomings. However, Ned's trust in us depends on our truth in all dealings. I am especially severe, while Marilyn tends to be more patient and sympathetic. This natural difference corresponds to what he wishes for in his parents, and allows me to indulge with impunity my tendency to criticize. As long as Marilyn is easy-going, he may learn better when antagonism is in the air.

Ned gleefully reports his doctor's disapproval of our challenges and pressures, hoping to play us off against him. He is only beginning to learn that "his" adults work cooperatively even with widely differing opinions. Exploring the weakest parts of his personality, the doctor finds Ned more enfeebled than do we, who look for stronger elements which we want to harness. Our expectations may stimulate growth without challenge to the doctor's accuracy.

Ned foments many crises before settling down to steady application. Wedded so long to disability, he cannot easily give up compulsions to wreck his own progress. In one more defiant gesture, he takes an extra week off after our winter vacation, knowing such absences are severely dealt with. Leaving us in the dark about his plans, he risks all he has achieved. When at last he returns with no excuse and incompleted algebra assignments, we lower the boom. Only when he agrees to accept an even heavier commitment in school, do we let him return.

Ned learns algebra, passes his examinations with a good grade, and returns to high school as a ninth grader. After graduating with honors, he goes to a well-known liberal arts college. He visits Marilyn from time to time and brings his friends as well as his brother, who he thinks needs our help. Many problems are still unsolved, but he has a better chance to dispose of them now that he can see the possibility of that ethical world he formerly discounted, for through the vision afforded by honesty in school life he is able to rediscover and mend the shattered fabric of a humanistic morality, naturally established on rational consideration and on respect and trust of others. With such values to lean on, Ned can and does accept the temporary limitations and restrictions teachers dare to lay upon him.

Matt's classroom behavior long continues to be dominated by sly, devious hostility; and persuading him to open up and directly express what he feels is a complicated, time-consuming process. Dreading the depth of his anger, Matt shies away from direct confrontations. We suspect murder in his heart. Seeking to channel his feelings into harmless currents we urge him to speak, to shout, to bang the table, to throw books, and slam doors.

He treats us like pharmakoi, pouring onto our heads the off-scourings of an agitated and unhappy childhood. A "difficult" twelve-year-old, he was sent away to boarding schools where his parents could keep him and his problems at a safe distance. Naturally he confuses his feelings about school with anger and sorrow over this early parental rejection. The boarding schools he hates were intended to be substitute families, as socially pretentious as his own. Heaping abuse upon them and teachers in general for conspiring against children and for being conniving tools of irresponsible parents, he has come to hate the fakery and snobbery that victimize him. Yet, he too plays the social climber's game, for looking down on others is an easy and familiar way of looking up at himself. Lifting education out of this tainted matrix is essential to any solution of his learning problems. Our most important step in that direction is to reject unearned associations and establish our identity.

We sympathize with his lonely struggles and can hardly help acting like parents for him. Yet the psychological material he is dredging up in psychotherapy makes it really urgent to fix in his mind the vast differences marking off parents, earlier teachers, and ourselves. Sometimes we feel that the doctor encourages him to work out his family feelings with and upon us, overriding our objections.

Matt is busy bringing a poisonous past to the surface. He works seriously, fighting hard and dirty, testing us over and over again. Each time he leaves school in anger and returns to discuss and work out his reasons, he does it on a grander scale. At last he is out for two weeks, and we fear he is giving up. But his doctor is working closely with him, and helps him decide. On re-entry, he is quiet for the first time, and seems largely drained of the false values and venomous fantasies he has carried with him for so long.

At last he is ready to see us as we are. He can and does absorb many of the values for which we stand. Gradually learning becomes attractive in itself. He undertakes the most routine, detailed chores, and starting from scratch he masters enough Spanish to go on later to a Spanish prize at his graduation from prep school. He studies with a spontaneity and relish that inspire other students to whom he now holds out a helping hand. He talks about planning to follow in our footsteps as a teacher of students with learning problems. "I know what they are," he says.

Matt is still in therapy, but his school problems are over and done with. After graduating from a large university he is in graduate school preparing to teach school himself. He calls us from time to time and visits with us, now as a close and valued friend. His own words summarize his experience at RSS and tell what happens with others as well:

While I attended Remedial Scholastic Services I experienced a series of valuable transitions in which I gained consciousness of myself as a student and as an individual. I consider this period the most important and significant part of my life. The changes in my values and objectives have helped me to be more aware of what I do and think, and have also made possible the completion of my high school education. I am now attending college and working for my degree.

In the spring of 1959 I left the boarding school I had attended for nearly two years. After the first year there I began to do very poor schoolwork, for I had become preoccupied with private thoughts, and I began to seriously oppose any academic obligations. The thoughts and problems of school and my family I lumped together, and I named school, teachers, administration, and rules all as my enemies. This mass hatred seemed so overwhelming and frightening that I dared not mention it in its entirety until quite a while after I had attended RSS. With this opposition to the idea of school and schoolwork and my consequent academic failure I entered RSS in the fall of 1959.

It is very difficult to be a fearful and suspicious individual in a school which emphasizes the exposure and understanding of inner feelings. Most of us in the school had deep secrets which were sometimes very distorted images of the truth, stemming from home or school experiences. Efforts of Mrs. Bernstein and Mr. Heinemann to help me understand my fears and reluctance I at first interpreted as threats to my personal life, for their questions and discussions seemed to tear at my private world. I at first thought of a change in my attitudes toward school as a potential loss of my personality. To replace one feeling with another was not so bad, but to totally drop a certain favorite defense was robbery! Before I was willing to give honest answers to their questions, I had to experiment, to think of a defense, perhaps a retaliation. Only later did I discover the feeling of quietness and relief which follows a spontaneously truthful answer to a question that dispels a fear.

There was a common conflict in the attitudes of most of the students toward improvement, which I term rejection and acceptance. No one at first readily and consistently accepted our teachers' help and advice. We would have to be certain of our friendships with Mrs. Bernstein and Mr. Heinemann before we exposed really vital and revealing problems. Yet the rejection of help would appear, I feel, as a fear of change, and an actual fear of doing well in school. Personal strength and independence were gratifying rewards for hard work and trust, but it was difficult to adjust my personality to the responsibilities which arose from independence and self-direction. Thus at any stage of our improvement we might feel that the going was too rough or that there was too much to do. I would often feel this when one improvement necessitated another, or when I was expected to work after clearing up a problem. Since Mrs. B and Mr. H emphasized the idea that improvement of behavior and schoolwork was really our decision, we often had conflicts between struggling on or quitting altogether. Many times I hesitated at the door of the school, trying to decide whether I should leave or stay, whether I should give up school or go on with the work of improvement. At these moments Mrs. Bernstein would plead with me to stay, and I would give her long and involved explanations of why it was no use to go on. But if I left, I returned because I felt a real need to continue. This inner desire to reach independence and strength was a motive which never left me, and it constitutes what I call acceptance.

Another conflict which I found difficult to deal with was my frequent feelings of intense anger. Anger was a problem to all of us. With the discussion of past experiences or when my teachers wanted me to explain my feelings, anger would well up inside me, sometimes leaving me speechless. These feelings and the fear of their dimensions had interfered with my learning throughout *all* my school experiences. At first my anger manifested itself in indirect and snide remarks, or I would turn it against myself and as a result become very depressed, and feel self-pity. A main objective of the school was to urge the student to talk freely about his anger, perhaps to see that it was not limitless, and could be understood. Through psychotherapy and discussions with my teachers I alleviated much frustration and depression. The energies which I dissipated on anger I learned to devote to schoolwork.

School was by no means a complete struggle! We read together Greek plays and mythology, other plays, novels, and articles. We often discussed literature or politics for hours at a time. I found that I could apply knowledge of myself to characters in plays and books. In general schoolwork ceased to be a series of problems and sheer obligations. On the contrary I found that the exchange of ideas, critical writing, and ancient history could be fascinating. I started to study Spanish and completed a first-year course on my own.

I found that the vast supplies of energy used for worry and anger can be transformed into a creative spirit; that knowing oneself and liking oneself is the greatest of all experiences after a period of doubt and unhappiness; and that if one feels that the world is barren of any happiness or possibilities, it is because he has not yet discovered any happiness within himself.

I feel that the real friendship which grew between my teachers and me was one of the most significant and wonderful aspects of school. Not only did I learn about myself and the feelings of *others*, but I also began to develop a critical eye. With self-understanding I am able to examine my environment, and to consciously choose those things which I really want. In short I progressed from the role of a mere pupil to that of a student.

X ❦ Conclusion

> *. . . there Leviathan*
> *Hugest of living Creatures, on the Deep*
> *Stretcht like a Promontory sleeps or swims,*
> *And seems a moving Land, and at his Gills*
> *Draws in, and at his Trunk spouts out a Sea.*

(*Paradise Lost*, Book VII, lines 412–416)

TODAY'S SCHOOLS DRAW in ever greater numbers of individuals plagued by learning disabilities; too many are spouted out again unimproved, or before their time. The fault lies not in the enormous size of the system but in its contradictory uses. Education as a promoter of social efficiency and uniformity is certainly today at odds with education as a path to knowledge and freedom.

In modern times Rousseau emphasized this antagonism between the individual and society. Jean-Jacques, goaded by the learning "blocks" of young pupils whom *he* had to teach, made the most brilliant plea for the education of free and creative individuals, and proclaimed the principle of natural learning. Since *Émile*, artists, thinkers, and occasionally even professional educators have locked horns with the dilemmas posed by rearing the "natural" child in a system leaning more and more heavily on the conditioned "unnatural." For two hundred years experimental schools have come and gone in Europe and America, each rephrasing the problems and offering answers. They are part of a noble and pervasive tradition.

Tolstoi and Bertrand Russell seem far removed from the romantic Rousseau, yet they ran schools to experiment with the meaning of all organized authority, looking hopefully to education as an instrument for radical social change. Others, equally opposed to brutal forcing, regimentation, and dehumanization, but less quixotic, have advocated practical modification instead of overthrow. RSS was pragmatic, arguing simply for a more natural teaching, consistent with an existing democratic school system.

The return to learning via the revival of a humane teacher-student relationship in the classroom is not a question of new methods or of revamping society's ideals. The work at RSS was remedial, not revolutionary; it can be introduced into public and private schools without resort to expensive teacher training or radical stargazing. It requires something more difficult, changes of attitude about learning and a rational appraisal of failure.

To deal openly with failure as a complicated problem in which the element of blame becomes irrelevant is only to face honestly what happens often during the course of all human life. The failure in school of an intelligent young person may be seen as a parental, a psychological, or a pedagogical failure, but in the face of the national obsession with academic success, failure can provide escape from the juggernaut. In this sense every student has a right to fail, a right to be recognized before the failure itself is to be understood or conjured away. Hasty denial in the name of positive thinking must yield to an acceptance of the total human condition. Even in an affluent society, room can and must be made for the expression of the negative sides of life.

Many excellent young people come to school in a weaker and more unformed state than they ought to. Everyone knows that children have to "adjust" to school discipline, but it is seldom understood until too late how devastating is the power of that discipline. The impact of the teacher's power on a self that knows nothing of its own sovereignty has a profound and sometimes shattering effect on learning. If this blow is not entirely responsible for learning disabilities, it is certainly the source of that intractability which nullifies the curative force of remedial techniques and baffles good intention. Authority is the reef upon which methods founder, even those engineered to cope with special problems. Reliance on such methods aggravates the disaster, because teachers may senselessly, even callously, ignore a crucial emotional issue which, while unresolved, inhibits and destroys natural relationships between student and teacher, between adolescent and adult. Whether defiant or outwardly compliant, the student will not or cannot be taught—though he may learn—until a relationship is restored. In severe cases like Larry's learning stops altogether.

To the brassy hostility of a troubled adolescent teachers often oppose either a show of force or a sweetly seductive disclaimer. Thus they block the undeveloped, hidden self, quivering behind its bravado, unconvinced. Though the student's available strength may be limited to a biological will to survive, his potential has a chance to unfold in school when teachers are sympathetically explicit about the purpose and extent of their authority. Until both are understood, there may be an intense fear of being overwhelmed by even such an impersonal discipline as subject-matter. The student's intractability reflects a childish willfulness, of course; it also may discover a pride and integrity that in alliance with the teacher's authority could deal with his problems.

Teaching authority originates in society's provisions for the education of the young, but in a democratic society that power is ineffectual as an educational instrument unless the young consciously agree they need it. Generally the groundwork for acceptance is laid long before adolescence, but this is not so with students incapable of sustaining self-confidence. These students raise the question as to why they are adversely affected by the teacher's ordinary exercise of authority, and who should be asked to help. Schools cannot run these problems out of the classroom into the psychotherapist's office where the doctor may softpedal or even deny his own authority, when he works with an individual. He can provide an environment entirely different from school, whereas teachers have no choice but to lead, instruct, and discipline, even when they emphasize the popular, and "new" inductive methods. When a school experience is the major factor in a learning problem, the student must pass through the fire that burns in the classroom to resolve the issue of school authority. It is true that the classroom teacher's most strenuous efforts will have little influence on learning disabilities rooted primarily in distorted family relationships. This does not justify the refusal of most schools to deal seriously with the problems of problem students.

Leading students to the issue of what to do with authority once they have decided to stay in school is a progressive series of actions and reactions, not a method or device to be mechanistically applied like phonics or "learning through games." There is no plan to manufacture graduated, small-scale ordeals to adjust to; actually, for some, all tasks at RSS were formidable. Our real design was to teach in whatever terms would convince students that school discipline and authority do not conspire against them, but work in partnership with their nature. The right pedagogical pressure offers to a person in transition a chance to borrow principles, ideas, and experience until he is strong enough to form his own. Thus, the teacher's temporary suzerainty stimulates growth and self-development. Explicit, articulate consciousness of its uses and of its goal, coupled with honest affection, breeds trust and approval. Firm governance complements the comradeship students feel within the school group. Unlike parental authority, this authority is contractual, always limited to academic learning.

In the end, a student's dogged determination to be healthy, his power to reason, and his growing and constructive self-awareness come from within and constitute the most important factors leading to success or failure. The student's realistic appraisal of his own strength and weakness allows the teacher's authority to help him learn academic subjects. Finally competent to follow his own inclinations, he can choose rebellion, conformity, or whatever compromise suits him.

We recognize that schools perpetuate social structures. They are not supposed to create or change them. Therefore we do not urge students to flout social conformity, even when it cramps their individual style, although at times we allowed such behavior within RSS. Moreover we admit that such prospects as nuclear warfare or the victory of material over spiritual aims indicate a depressingly gloomy future to all youth. Some, of course, must regard any positive effort as tarnished or suspect. All the same, most can work with what exists to make a successful return to learning.

Our democracy has room for individuals who are offended, frustrated, or disillusioned by contemporary trends. Is it not reasonable, then, to ask the school reflecting and sustaining this society to give them an honorable place in the system? By respecting their authentic dissent the school gives intelligent students a chance to make the best use of education as they find it, avoiding or clearing up learning disabilities on their own.

At RSS we found that there are effective alternatives to dronelike skill building and subhuman training for efficiency. RSS argues the restorative values of trusting and honest relationships, intelligent, straightforward, and sympathetic answers to the democratic protests of the bright ones who fail.